FUNNY QUOTES

NUMEROUS OCCASIONS

Geoffrey Lamb

DAVID & CHARLES
Newton Abbot   London
North Pomfret (Vt)

Thomas Hardy wrote Tess of the Dormobiles.

I married beneath me. All women do.

Mary had a little lamb – the midwife fainted.

'Rabbit hutch wanted for old peoples' home'

Evan Morgan taught an Australian parakeet to creep up his trouser leg and poke its head out through his fly-buttons.

British Library Cataloguing in Publication Data

Funny quotes: for numerous occasions.
1. Quotations, English
I. Lamb, G.F.
080   PN6081
ISBN 0-7153-9151-8

Photoset in Linotron Sabon by
Northern Phototypesetting Co, Bolton
and printed in Great Britain
by Billings Ltd, Worcester
for David & Charles Publishers plc
Brunel House Newton Abbot Devon

Published in the United States of America
by David & Charles Inc
North Pomfret Vermont 05053 USA

DEDICATIONS

To any friend I have left in Ireland after the publication of this book.

(Up the Rebels) George A. Birmingham

For DURRELL – My Favourite Beast.

(Beasts in My Bed) Jacquie Durrell (wife of Gerald Durrell)

To scrambled eggs on toast this book is affectionately dedicated.

(Book of Worries) Robert Morley

To my daughter Leonora, without whose never-failing sympathy and encouragement this book would have been finished in half the time.

(Heart of a Goof) P. G. Wodehouse

Age

A witness cannot give evidence of his age unless he can remember being born.

(Judge) John Blagden

No woman should ever be quite accurate about her age. It looks so calculating.

Oscar Wilde

OLD AGE

Old age is the happiest time in a man's life. The worst of it is, there's so little of it.

W. S. Gilbert

If I'd known I was going to live so long I'd have taken better care of myself.

Leon Eldred

Avoid school reunions. The last man I met who was at school with me had a long white beard and no teeth.

P. G. Wodehouse

No man is ever old enough to know better. *Holbrook Jackson*

I'm in the prime of senility. *J. Chandler Harris*

Age is a very high price to pay for maturity. *Tom Stoppard*

'Rabbit hutch wanted for old people's home.' (Advertisment in Middlesex local paper)

The Daily Telegraph

HOW TO BE A CENTENARIAN

On her 107th birthday she attributed her great age to the fact that she had never had a boyfriend.

The Star

America

America is a mistake, a giant mistake. *Sigmund Freud*

It's the land of permanent waves and impermanent wives.

Brendan Behan

Air-conditioned land-cruisers, drenched in Musak, with Coca-Cola available from a tap in the dashboard.

Patrick Campbell

By having so many tons of metal hurtling along . . . hooting, winking, overtaking, they hoped to convince themselves and one another that they were important.

Kingsley Amis

What this country's got is beautifully packaged inefficiency.

Alfred Grossman

America is a large friendly dog in a small room. Every time it wags its tail it knocks over a chair.

Arnold Toynbee

The Americans, hard as they may now find it to stomach the fact, are basically English. After all, we invented them.

Arthur Marshall

Thousands of American women know more about the Subconscious than they know about plain sewing.

H. L. Mencken

The terrible newly-imported American doctrine that everybody ought to do something.

Osbert Sitwell

Anger

People in a temper often say a lot of silly, terrible things that they really mean.

Penelope Gilliatt

Becoming angry makes me furious.   *Richard Gordon*

I could see that, if not actually disgruntled, he was far from being gruntled.

P. G. Wodehouse

Animals

MAN AND BEAST

I don't mind an animal sharing my bed, but I strongly object to being woken up at five o'clock in the morning by an enthusiastic squirrel trying to push a peanut in my ear.

Gerald Durrell

Most of the zoos I have ever visited were horrible smelly places where I wouldn't dream of keeping a dead cat.

Jacquie Durrell

Monkeys have terrible toilet habits – terrible to us, that is.

Bruce Fogle

LOWER ANIMALS

'You act like an animal' is in a way a sort of compliment if by that you mean any animal other than man.

Mike Harding

New Zealand, as a professor once said, is a country of thirty million sheep, three million of whom think they're human beings!

Barry Humphries

Humans show their superiority to the lower animals by their ability to invent. They have invented, for example, rifles, machine guns, high explosive bombs, poison gas, and nuclear weapons.

Lambert Jeffries

CRITICAL EYE

A camel took charge of my overcoat and examined it with a critical eye, as if he had an idea of getting one made like it.

Mark Twain

The steady supercilious eye of a frog resembled that of a bishop at the Athenaeum inspecting a shy new member.

P. G. Wodehouse

TALK AND TRAINING

There are limits to the conversation one can have with a parrot.

Peter Ustinov

Dolphins are so intelligent that within a few days of captivity they have trained humans to stand at the side of a pool and throw fish to them.

Anon

ANIMAL LIFE – AND DEATH

The cow is of the bovine ilk;
One end is moo, the other milk.

Ogden Nash

The fox lets its home get foul with old bones and feathers. Foxes probably smoke in bed as well.

John Tickner

A sort of gulpy, gurgly, plobby, squishy, wofflesome sound, like a thousand eager men drinking soup in a foreign restaurant. The Empress (champion sow) was feeding.

P. G. Wodehouse

'Sausages from pigs that die happy! A delicious speciality!'
(Advertisement in Hampshire paper)

This England

WILD LIFE

To me, a hippopotamus is beautiful. I much prefer them to swans.

Henry Moore

If strolling forth, a beast you view
Whose hide with spots is peppered,
As soon as it has lept on you
You'll know it is a leopard.

Carolyn Wells

MICE AND MEN

How many mice had Burns studied before deciding that their best-laid schemes gang aft a-gley?

Auberon Waugh

W. R. Hearst [American newspaper proprietor] loved animals . . .
When the dining-hall became infested with mice, far from destroying them, he left out tasty titbits for them.

David Niven

Army

The marksmanship was excellent. The shooting of the regimental sergeant-major was especially satisfactory.

Daily Express

Once you have sworn allegiance to Queen and Country, it becomes illegal to lose things, especially firearms.

Clement Freud

A Jewish Army recruit, asked by his commanding officer if he would like a commission, replied, 'No thank you, sir, I'd rather have a straight salary'.

Benny Lee

My medical consisted of a doctor who had obviously been dead a month. He asked me two questions: (1) Have you got piles? (2) Any insanity in the family? I answered Yes to both and was accepted A1.

Spike Milligan

Art

Buy Old Masters. They fetch a much better price than old mistresses.

Lord Beaverbrook

He filled the drawing-room with priceless pictures – acting on the principle that one good Turner deserves another.

Harry Graham

Corot painted over three thousand pictures. At least ten thousand of them are in America.

Anon

An Australian gentleman considered making me an offer for my Rembrandt. But another member of his group said, 'Don't bother, Jack. We've already got a Rembrandt in Australia'.

Duke of Bedford

A work of art is useless. So is a flower.   *Oscar Wilde*

MODERN ART

What is there to bite on in the abstract? You might as well eat triangles.

Joyce Cary

One sees a square lady with three breasts and a guitar up her crotch.

Noel Coward

My audience mustn't know whether I'm spoofing or being serious. I mustn't know either.

Salvador Dali

Dali decided to have a one-man show, which he did, and it was a great success. One man showed up.

Woody Allen

One reassuring thing about modern art is that things can't be as bad as they're painted.

Walthall Jackson

The beautiful doesn't matter to me.   *Pablo Picasso*

TECHNIQUE

Painting is easy when you don't know how, but difficult when you do.

Edgar Degas

AUDACITY

An art student, wishful for wider recognition of his talents, strode bravely into the National Gallery . . . and hung up one of his own paintings. It is said to have remained there for seventeen days before anybody, other than art lovers, noticed it.

Arthur Marshall

Babies

A loud voice at one end and no sense of responsibility at the other.
E. Adamson

A baby is a misshapen creature of no particular age, sex, or condition.
Ambrose Bierce

Babies are so human – they remind one of monkeys.
Saki

The baby was healthy and fat, and looked no more and no less like a raw beetroot than any other baby.
A. G. MacDonell

Out of the mouths of babes come things you wouldn't want your neighbour to hear.
H. Meade

When babies arrive at our house, I try to be asleep.*Robert Morley*

An extra font is being added near the chancel, so that babies can be baptised at both ends.
Parish Magazine

Mary had a little lamb – the midwife fainted.
Leonard Rossiter

BEFORE AND AFTER

Many women still believe that if they want a male child, the husband should wear boots at the time of the conception.
Anon

When you've just had a baby you're like a zombie . . . a walking milk bottle.
Avril Silver

Almost anyone can look after a baby. The demanding phase of parenthood begins when they *stop* being babies.
Mary Kenny

Ballet

There is always an injury from which a ballerina is either just recovering or by which she has just been struck down.
Nicholas Drumgoole

Members of the public have asked wonderingly, 'What do you do all day?'
Nicholas Drumgoole

All those great swans chasing that absurd young man!
Terence Rattigan

In less inspired moments Isadora Duncan followed the music as a bear might pursue a mouse.

Adrian Stokes

Bastards

I called him a love child by another name.   *Tina Spencer Knott*

Everyone is proud of being a bastard here [Chicago].   *Saul Bellow*

Beauty

Beauty is generally a proud, vain, saucy, expensive, impertinent sort of commodity.

Charles Macklin

Her chin is absolutely right. It forms a gentle, graceful point, balanced between wide eyes.

Birmingham Weekly News

Tall and dark with large eyes, a perfect profile, and an equally perfect figure, she was an oriental potentate's dream of what the harem needed.

P. G. Wodehouse

Bed

Much credit has been given to the anonymous inventor of the wheel. But what of the anonymous inventor of the bed?

Peg Bracken

I always think a bed that hasn't been slept in looks sort of forlorn in the morning.

John Van Druten

BED MANNERS

Lady Capricorn, he understood, was still keeping open bed.

Aldous Huxley

One good turn gets most of the blanket.   *Reader's Digest*

A young African lady broke off her engagement when she learnt that her fiancé took his clothes off when he went to bed.

Mary Eden and Richard Carrington

One of the hazards of going to bed with a gentleman is that he often shares it with one or more of his dogs.

Douglas Sutherland

EARLY TO RISE

If, for any urgent reason, I ought to be up particularly early in the morning, it is then that I love to lie an extra half-hour in bed.

J. K. Jerome

Bewilderment

He stood there feeling like Romeo if Juliet had shoved him off the balcony.

Richard Gordon

Birds

'I can never find a site to suit me,' said the cuckoo. 'Either there's no view, or the water's bad, or I dislike the neighbours.'

E. V. Lucas

The wise thrush sings each song twice over because he can't get it right first time.

Robert Robinson

Boats

We knew nothing at all about sailing, except that you wear white hats for it.

J. B. Boothroyd

Big motor launches go towering past . . . sending your frying-pan sliding into the scuppers – whatever they are.

J. B. Boothroyd

I once took my family for a peaceful holiday in a motor-cruiser on the Thames. I found it like driving up the M1 on a bank holiday, with no brakes.

Richard Gordon

At the boating lake at Hove, if you are gone more than five minutes a boatman comes out and gets you. You could be gone five years on the Broads, and no one would worry but the insurance company.

J. B. Boothroyd

'The buoys marking the shoals are often out of position, so mariners are cautioned to be on their guard.' (Official notice at Corfu)

Gerald Durrell

Body

'You want to say: look, this body's doesn't really suit me. Could I move into something different? But you can't. The body's a tied cottage.'

Alan Bennett

Researchers have proved that liars can control other parts of their body but generally forget about their feet. A liar can never stand still.

Diana Dors

The sweeping, criss-crossing ligaments of the pelvis in Figure 341 [Gray's *Anatomy*] indicate what our Maker could have done with motorway junctions.

Richard Gordon

It's ungrammatical to talk about putting your best foot forward unless you're a quadruped.

Lambert Jeffries

The last reflection of my figure that I saw in a glass was so disagreeable, I resolved to spare myself such mortification in the future.

Mary Wortley Montagu

He [Aleister Crowley] was bald as a stone, and his huge expanse of naked hairless yellowish face was faintly suggestive of an enormous penis.

Maurice Richardson

Books

There is no more merit in having read a thousand books than in having ploughed a thousand fields.

W. Somerset Maugham

You may write an excellent book which will be reviewed at length in the quality newspapers and weeklies – in other words, it will remain unnoticed.

George Mikes

It is estimated that a good bishop, denouncing [a book] from the pulpit with the right organ note in his voice, can add between fifteen and twenty thousand to the sales.

P. G. Wodehouse

When I asked Harvey Smith to choose one book to take to the desert island, he laughed and said he had never read a book in his life.

Roy Plomley

'Five thousand books wanted by gentleman for recently purchased country house, to fill library. Subjects immaterial.'
(Advertisement in South Buckinghamshire newspaper)

This England

Leave my book [*Dorian Gray*], I beg you, to the immortality it deserves.

Oscar Wilde

Boredom

I rose politely in the Club
And said, 'I feel a little bored;
Will someone take me to a pub?'   *G. K. Chesterton*

There are times when any normal person will be bored – for instance, during committee meetings, or watching Boycott bat.

Tim Heald

We can forgive those who bore us; we cannot forgive those whom we bore.

La Rochefoucald

I'm good at getting away from people who bore me. I'm not rude; I just run for it.

Françoise Sagan

Buildings

The higher the buildings the lower the morals.   *Noel Coward*

'Have you seen the buildings he's putting up? Half his tenants are asking to be rehoused, and they haven't even moved in yet.'

Alan Ayckbourn

I thought it [Sydney Opera House] looked as if it was something that had crawled out of the sea and was up to no good.

Beverley Nichols

Business

My boss called me into the office and said, 'You're fired'. I thought that was a good time to quit the job.

Derek Dingle

Nowadays twenty-one is almost over the threshold of middle age for young executives.

Spike Hughes

If in any doubt, file under H for 'Haven't a Clue'.   *Roger Kilroy*

When a man is in his cups his suspicion is asleep . . . Can there be a happier moment than that to strike a bargain?

Charles Macklin

Cars
CARS OLD AND NEW

The car of tomorrow is being driven on the highway of yesterday by the driver of today.

Rolfe Arrow

It's difficult not to feel sorry for derelict cars.   *Virginia Graham*

An old car that is going well will continue to do so until you fit it with four new tyres.

Leonard Rossiter

Motor cars have never been quite the same for me since people stopped winding them up at the front with a handle.

Arthur Marshall

People don't want a cheaper car. They want an expensive car that costs less.

Anon

MOTORING MANNERS

All power corrupts, and horse-power corrupts absolutely.

John Hillaby

There is no more irresistible mating call than the imperious horn at the kerb.

Bergen Evans

Don't come so close. I hardly know you.

(Rear-window car sticker)

DRIVERS IN DISMAY

Slip the edge of your offside tyre over a continuous white line in an empty lane at four o'clock in the morning, and a squad car immediately pops up out of the long grass.

Patrick Campbell

It is well-known that if you stop and wind the window down to ask someone the way, he invariably turns out to be either deaf, senile, or a stranger.

Lambert Jeffries

When I press the brake pedal the headlights go on and a voice
speaks from the steering-wheel.

Spike Milligan

A lorry carrying onions has overturned on the M1. Motorists are
asked to find a hard shoulder to cry on.

Gyles Brandreth

Do driving examiners all have to imitate a Dalek when they speak?
'Please. Turn. Left. At. The. Next. Available. Turning.'

Mary Kenny

Cats

With cats, some say, one rule is true:
Don't speak till you are spoken to.

T. S. Eliot

Mr Dick justly observed to me . . . 'You know, Trotwood, I don't
want to swing a cat.'

Charles Dickens

I am not a cat man, but a dog man, and all felines can tell this at a
glance – a sharp vindictive glance.

James Thurber

Charity

Faith, hope, and charity, and the greatest of these is charity – if
you're on the receiving end.

Lambert Jeffries

No one likes charity – it makes them wince.   *Paul McCartney*

Children

Have you ever had that sneaking feeling that shop-keepers don't
like children?

Serena Allott

It was no wonder people were so horrible when they started life as
children.

Kingsley Amis

He finished his drink with a silent toast to Herod. *Kingsley Amis*

Children keep you exhausted. That's half the point of them.

Martin Amis

There is much to be learnt from that piece of advice printed on most bottles of patent medicine: 'Keep Away from Small Children'. Personally I've always avoided them as much as possible.   *Denis Norden*

The trouble with children is that they are not returnable.
                                                    Quentin Crisp

I think I was popular with my teachers . . . on Saturdays and Sundays.
                                                    Eric Morecambe

'I've never been able to bear with fortitude anything in the shape of a kid with golden curls.'
                                                    P. G. Wodehouse

CHILD CARE

The first act of many child experts is to hire a nanny.
                                                    Lynette Burrows

Many people prefer children to dogs, principally, I think, because a licence is not required for the former.
                                                    Harry Graham

Every child should have an occasional pat on the back – as long as it is applied low enough and hard enough.
                                                    Fulton J. Sheen

The kidnappers take me to New Jersey, bound and gagged, and my parents finally realize that I'm kidnapped and they snap into action immediately . . . They rent out my room.
                                                    Woody Allen

I spent most of my time standing in the corner with a wet diaper on my head.
                                                    Peter Ustinov

To watch a little child drowning within a few yards of me has a dispiriting effect upon my appetite.
                                                    Harry Graham

MOTHER LOVE

My mother loved children. She would have given anything if I had been one.   *Groucho Marx*

She once sent to the nursery for a child to take to church. 'Which child, madam?' 'How should I know? Whichever one goes best with my blue dress.' (Mrs Willie James – bastard daughter of Edward VII)
                                                    Maurice Richardson

CHILDISH WAYS

I love little children, but *not* in the train.   *Joyce Grenfell*

The doorstep of a busy shop is the place they always select for sitting down and taking off their shoes.

J. K. Jerome

Children do not have psychology. They have nasty habits. All of which are inherited from your spouse's side of the family.

Richard Gordon

Prodigy – a child who plays the piano when he ought to be in bed.

J. B. Morton

We've had bad luck with our children – they've all grown up.

Christopher Morley

If I knew an honest schoolboy, I would begin to count my silver spoons as he grew up.

Arnold Bennett

In my younger years I was a motor-car . . . I switched on in the morning, and only stopped being a car at night, when I reversed into bed.

Peter Ustinov

Christmas

Mistletoe is fast disappearing now people have sex all the year round.

Cecil Dixon (Covent Garden agent)

The tree is shedding every one of its needles on the carpet, and the cards all fall over every time anyone opens a door.

Virginia Graham

For guests who overstay their welcome at Christmas Auberon Waugh has 'a Californian wine of indescrible filth . . . tasting of nail varnish with an undertow of diesel exhaust'.

Anthea Hall

There should be Christmas laws: (1) It is forbidden to spend more than £2 on any person. (2) One is *not* obliged to kiss any woman under the mistletoe. (3) Christmas cards must be sent only to close relatives.

Spike Milligan

There's a perv in Soho who dresses up as Father Christmas, then solicits strangers: 'Merry Christmas – want to see a Christmas porn-film?'

Spike Milligan

Cinema

This Oscar thing is a sort of popularity test. When it's your turn you win it.

Woody Allen

At Southport the magistrates decided that during the Jubilee celebrations children over fourteen should be allowed to see films licensed for adults only.

Evening Standard

Strip away the phoney tinsel of Hollywood and you'll find the real tinsel underneath.

Oscar Levant

The shooting of the Korda film about Nelson was held up because nobody could remember which arm he lost.

Arthur Marshall

After listening to Samuel Goldwin expatiating about the art of making pictures, Bernard Shaw closed the conversation by saying, 'That's the difference between us; you talk of art, Mr Goldwyn, while I think of money'.

Divid Niven

Civil Service

The way some Civil Servants talk you'd think God was in another department.

Brendan Behan

Rule A: Your boss is never wrong.
Rule B: If you discover he *is* wrong, refer to Rule A.   *Anon*

Class

The Irish Terrier I owned would differentiate between the guests, in whom he displayed a courteous interest, and the servants, whom he treated with polite indifference.

James Wentworth Day

We don't like being regarded as Suburbia. Most of us will fix the number on the gate, but we won't put it on our notepaper. (Indignant resident whose street was allotted numbers)

The Times

Striking stevedores rejected an appeal to unload 41 tons of melons going over-ripe. The melon, they said, is not a working man's fruit.

This England

You can be in the Horse Guards and still be common.

Terence Rattigan

There is no anguish so acute as that experienced by a hostess who mistakes a member of her staff for a scion of the nobility.

P. G. Wodehouse

To the Christian there is no class distinction. The fact that the best families sit in the front pews is just a matter of tradition.

Anon

Clothes

MENSWEAR

My ill-fitting tweed suit . . . had apparently been made to measure for an under-nourished gorilla.

Kingsley Amis

There were stands of shoes and sandals too ugly not to be hand-made.

Kingsley Amis

We let ourselves be told what taxis we can or can't take by a man at a hotel door, simply because he has a drum-major's uniform on.

Robert Benchley

In three days he can make the newest suit look like a bagful of bulbs.

A. P. Herbert

One of the more depressing experiences of middle life . . . is trying on your old RAF uniform and finding that the only part that still fits you is the tie.

Denis Norden

BOOTS AND SHOES

A shoe shop in New York sports a sign which says: 'Our boots cover a multitude of shins'.

The Daily Telegraph

WOMEN'SWEAR

When she raises her eyelids it's just as if she were taking off all her clothes.

Colette

Every time a woman leaves off something she looks better.

Will Rogers

In her dark green dress, with the low-cut rounded neckline, he saw that she had lovely legs.

G. H. Coxe

My clothes seem to suffer a sea-change when they get on to me. They look quite promising in the shop.

Joyce Grenfell

High heels were invented by a woman who had been kissed on the forehead.

Christopher Morley

President Marcos fled the Philippines leaving behind his wife's wardrobe – including 2,700 pairs of shoes.

Sunday Telegraph Magazine

She was stark naked except for a PVC raincoat, dress, net stockings, undergarments, shoes, rain hat, and gloves.

Keith Waterhouse

Clubs

I wouldn't want to belong to a club that would have me as a member.

Groucho Marx

Most clubs have the atmosphere of a Duke's house with the Duke lying dead upstairs.

Douglas Sutherland

Cookery

The successful boiling of an egg can sometimes be an almost impossible achievement.

Spike Hughes

Those who make omelettes properly can do nothing else.

Hilaire Belloc

The most famous Coarse Cook in English history used to burn cakes instead of baking them.

Spike Hughes

Countryside

In order to preserve the natural beauty of the countryside, parking space was made available for no more than thirty thousand cars.

Alan Coren

Cricket

Spinners have an advantage over fast bowlers because they can go on until they qualify for the old age pension.

Fred Trueman

The only qualification a man needs to become a first-class cricketer is Yorkshire blood in his veins.

Ernie Wise

Fast bowlers enjoy bad light, and never have any difficulty in picking out the shape of the stumps or the batman's skull.

A. B. Hollowood

If a fast bowler is allowed to strike a batsman on the head with the ball, why shouldn't the batsman be allowed to retaliate by giving the bowler a crack on the head with the bat?

Lambert Jeffries

Not long ago Harvey-Walker, the Derbyshire batsman, announced his opinion of a brutal wicket at Buxton by striding to the middle and handing over his false teeth to the square-leg umpire.

Michael Parkinson

I am not saying that it is necessary for a fast bowler to be a homicidal maniac, but it certainly helps.

Michael Parkinson

They set me up as an untameable northern savage who ate broken glass and infant batsmen for breakfast.

Fred Trueman

At Leicester two years ago, I'm told, I welcomed listeners with the words, 'You've come in at a very appropriate time – Ray Illingworth has just relieved himself at the pavilion end'.

Brian Johnston

Crime

People always leave their hall lights on to deter burglars – I don't know why. I mean, there can be very few households who actually choose to spend their evenings sitting in the hall with the rest of the house in darkness.

Alan Ayckbourn

'I forget the punishment for compassing the death of the Heir Apparent. . . I know it's something humorous, but lingering, with either boiling oil or melted lead.'

W. S. Gilbert

The torso in the trunk . . . is a type of crime which has diminished with the spread of airline luggage, in which you couldn't conceal a chopped rabbit.

Richard Gordon

You can get much farther with a kind word and a gun than you can with a kind word alone.

Al Capone

If England treats her criminals the way she has treated me, she doesn't deserve to have any.

Oscar Wilde

Critics

CRITICAL COMMENT

The play's impact was like the banging together of two damp dish-cloths.

Brendan Behan

Mrs Ruppert is unfortunately not an actress at all . . . but her pathos is deliciously comic.

R. E. Golding Bright

The third movement [of Bartok's Fourth Quartet] began with a dog howling at midnight, proceeded to imitate the regurgitations of the less refined type of water-closet and concluded with the cello reproducing the screech of an ungreased wheelbarrow.

Alan Dent

Gertrude Stein was masterly in making nothing happen very slowly.

Clifton Fadiman

Mr Clarke played the King [in *King Lear*] as though under constant apprehension that someone else was about to play the ace.

Eugene Field

Turner's painting 'The Slave Ship' resembles a tortoise-shell cat having a fit in a plate of tomatoes.

Mark Twain

CRITICS UNDER FIRE

Critics are like eunuchs: they've seen it done, they know how it should be done, but they can't do it themselves.

Brendan Behan

Criticism is like an airport – acceptable as long as it's not in my direction.   *Geoff Donald*

This review has the place of honour in my lavatory.

David Niven

A critic is a legless man who teaches running.

Channing Pollock

I have just read your lousy review buried in the back pages of the paper. I have never met you, but if I do you'll need a new nose.

Harry Truman (American President addressing the music critic of the *Washington Post*)

Don't you loathe the critics? Their mere existence seems to me an impertinence.

P. G. Wodehouse

When Liberace has attracted critical venom he has fallen back on his catchphrase, 'I cried all the way to the bank', which he later capped with, 'and then I bought the bank'.

Martyn Harris

I don't believe it. Even *The Times* likes it!

Terence Rattigan (on *French Without Tears*)

He quoted dead languages to hide his ignorance of life.

Beerbohm Tree (on A. B. Walkley, dramatic critic of *The Times*)

Dancing

The room is filled with the sound of an interminable Scottish reel which plays without a break.

Alan Ayckbourn

The music is so loud you can't chat anyone up. Everybody dances apart without touching anyone else, so presumably they all go home alone.

Mike Harding (on disco dancing)

Peter Townsend once had, as in a fearful nightmare, to teach Queen Mary how to dance the Hokey Cokey.

Arthur Marshall

On one famous occasion Pavlova was asked how she danced. She replied that if she could put it into words she wouldn't dance.

Kathy O'Shaughnessy

I've been locked in his noxious embrace for the 35 years this waltz has lasted. Will that orchestra never stop?

Dorothy Parker

'If you must be a wallflower, dear, don't take root. Move around a little.'

Peg Bracken

Death
THE BRIGHT SIDE

Dying is one of the few things that can be done just as easily lying down.

Woody Allen

Funeral: a pageant whereby we show our respect for the dead by enriching the undertaker.

Ambrose Bierce

The fence around a cemetery is foolish, for those inside will never come out and those outside don't want to get in.

Arthur Brisbane

To die is to leave off dying and do the thing once and for all.

Samuel Butler

Last Will and Testament: I, being of sound mind and body, have spent every penny.

Ray Ellington

There are many people walking about who would be much more interesting dead.

Richard Gordon

You can't say civilization don't advance. In every war they kill you a new way.

Will Rogers

My Irish grandmother made death her life work. *Hugh Leonard*

What I look forward to is not a violent death, but dying in the normal way, with my head in the gas oven.

Lee Pavia

I should like to die in Manchester. The transition between Manchester and death would be almost unnoticeable.

Lord Rosebery

THE DARK SIDE

'I'd hate to drown. You look so awful afterwards.'

Alan Ayckbourn

Dying can damage your health. Every coffin contains a Government health warning.

Spike Milligan

Early to rise and early to bed makes a male healthy and wealthy and dead.

James Thurber

Dying in Paris is really a very difficult and expensive luxury for a foreigner.

Robert Ross

There's no bad publicity except an obituary. *Brendan Behan*

My grandfather was a very insignificant man. At his funeral the hearse followed the other cars.

Woody Allen

Parishioners are requested to cut the grass around their own graves.

Parish Magazines

He who dies of a surfeit is as dead as he who starves.

James Thurber

IMMORTAL LONGINGS

I don't want to achieve immortality through my work. I want to achieve it through not dying.

Woody Allen

Millions of people long for immortality though they don't know what to do with themselves on a rainy Sunday afternoon.

Susan Ertz

Eternity is a terrible thought. I mean, where's it going to end?

Tom Stoppard

He had decided to live for ever or die in the attempt.

Joseph Heller

Do not try to live for ever. You will not succeed.

George Bernard Shaw

Defeat

Victory has a hundred memories but defeat has amnesia.

W. I. Gates

Dentists

Said the dentist to the mother of a fractious child patient: 'That filling is still fresh, so don't let him bite anyone for at least three hours.'

Reader's Digest

A toothache can sometimes be cured by laying out a few old copies of *Punch* on your dining-table.

Huw Wheldon

Diplomacy

A diplomat is a fellow that lets you do all the talking while he gets what he wants.

Kin Hubbard

When a diplomat says yes, he means perhaps; when he says perhaps, he means no; and when he says no, he is no diplomat.

Leonard Rossiter

A diplomat is a person who can tell you to go to hell in such a way that you actually look forward to the trip.

Caskie Stinnet

Divorce

Divorce is when a husband no longer has to bring the money home to the wife. He can mail it.

Morty Craft

Marriage is the first step towards divorce.   *Pamela Mason*

A Bermudian wife, in seeking a divorce, insisted to the magistrate that her grounds were simple and sufficient. 'I have reason to believe that my husband is not the father of my last child.'

James Thurber

Doctors

'So it goes on. Day after day. Week after week. They troop in with their sore throats and varicose veins . . . Is this the image of God, this sagging parcel of vanilla blancmange hoisted day after day on to the consulting-room table?'   (Dr Wicksteed), *Alan Bennett*

I don't mind his going into medicine as long as his medicine doesn't go into me.

W. S. Gilbert

Doctors in books never get more than four hours' sleep on any night of the year.

E. M. Delafield

Not many people have the luck to consult a psychiatrist and come out on the winning side.

Richard Gordon

The conventional doctor views the public as a bunch of feckless, self-indulgent, dim-witted lead-swingers.

Richard Gordon

'This doctor said that when he wrote out a prescription for pills, it was no different from what they did in the old days when they recited a spell.'

Michael Frayn

You can catch more things in doctors' waiting rooms than you go in with.

Mike Harding

Drink

It's called a miniature cocktail: drink one and in a minute you're out.

Roger Allen

To my palate the sherry tasted like the brine pickled herrings are bottled in, plus a scintilla of dishcloth.

Kinglsey Amis

I must step out of these wet things and into a dry martini.

Robert Benchley

Nobody knows what they're drinking. If you give it a high sounding name and charge enough for it, they'll think it's marvellous.

Henry Cecil

This much-treasured brew looked like weak milk, smelt like burning rubber, and tasted like nothing I could possibly describe. (The palm wine of Bafut)

Jacquie Durrell

WHISKY GALORE

You can have any drink you like as long as it's whisky.

Derek Bates

He almost ate his glass of whisky, so savagely did he attack it.

Patrick Campbell

I've been told that the effect of whisky on the human body is very serious, but I've found that the effect of absence of whisky is even worse.

W. C. Fields

WINE-BIBBERS

You mustn't hurry wine. Wine is like a woman – she is never ready when you want to go out.

Miles Kington

Our absurdly small wine list contains only twenty-three choices of champagne. (Suggestions Book of a London club)
Arthur Marshall

Port wine will be supplied to those who are teetotallers, in accordance with a well-known English custom.
The Times

BEER-BIBBER

'Beer-drinking don't do half the harm of love-making.'
Eden Phillpotts

OVER THE EIGHT

I drink like a fish. The only difference is that we drink different stuff.
Brendan Behan

There is a certain social barrier between the drunk and the sober which it is very difficult to bridge.
Michael Frayn

I always keep a supply of stimulant handy in case I see a snake — which I also keep handy.
W. C. Fields

He has a hole under his nose that all his money goes into.
Thomas Fuller

A beautiful blonde once drove me to drink. It's the only good thing she did.
W. C. Fields

An alcoholic is someone you don't like who drinks as much as you do.
Dylan Thomas

You're not drunk if you can lie on the floor without holding on.
Dean Martin

COFFEE FOR CONNOISSEURS

She insisted on making coffee by a Hungarian method that included blowing down the mouth of the pot.
Maurice Richardson

CLEANERS' CUPPA

The waiter's reaction when I asked for tea instead of coffee after a meal was, 'No, we don't do tea, but the cleaners drink it. Maybe I can find one of their tea-bags'.
Anthea Hall

Eccentrics

Sir Sydney Smith was an eccentric pathologist, who woke his Edinburgh students by firing revolvers.

Richard Gordon

The Duke of St Albans refused to be moved from a hotel that had at breakfast time caught fire and was merrily blazing. ('Rubbish! Bring me some more toast!')

Arthur Marshall

Evan Morgan taught an Australian parakeet to creep up his trouser leg and poke its head out through his fly-buttons.

Maurice Richardson

I left the mess in some alarm when a visiting air commodore ate a champagne glass whole, stem and all.

David Niven

He refereed one of our games holding up an umbrella to keep the teeming rain off his head.

Geoffrey Green

Over one hundred years ago a man in Worcester had eaten fifty-two pounds of plums at one sitting.

Dylan Thomas

RELATIVES

Our relatives are all either fossilized or mental. There's Great Uncle Patrick, who wanders about nude and tells complete strangers how he killed whales with a penknife.

Gerald Durrell

My grandmother had a close relationship with a small red squirrel . . . She was convinced that it was the reincarnation of a much-loved cousin.

Joyce Grenfell

Every night, when my father comes home, he gets out a pistol and shouts 'Hitler! If you're in this house, come out with your hands up!' *Spike Milligan*

ROUND THE BEND

I am independent; *you* are eccentric; *he* is round the bend.
Anthony Jay and Jonathan Lynn

An eccentric is a person too rich or too powerful to be called crazy.
Eve Pollard

Economics

A study of economics reveals that the best time to buy anything is last year.

Marty Allen

The love of economy is the root of all virtue.

George Bernard Shaw

He used the old-fashioned mangle for getting the last scrap of toothpaste out of the tube.

Frank Muir

Economy is going without something you want in case some day you might want something else you probably won't want.

Anthony Hope

Wherever there exists a demand, there is *no* supply. *Oscar Wilde*

One man's pay rise is another man's price increase.

Harold Wilson

Everybody is always in favour of general economy and particular expenditure.

Anthony Eden

Education

British education is probably the best in the world if you can survive it.

Peter Ustinov

How long would it take six men to build a wall if three of them took a week? I recall that we spent almost as much time on this problem as the men spent on the wall.

Gerald Durrell

PARENTS

If I stood up and told the parents that I wasn't trying to produce leaders of men, they'd throw rotten apples.

Ian Beer (Headmaster of Harrow School)

The parent who 'wants a word with Teacher' usually comes armed with a good many words, most of them bad ones. *Balaam*

PROGRESS UNSATISFACTORY

She has set herself an extremely low standard, which she has failed to maintain.

(School report on *Jilly Cooper*)

'This boy will go far. The sooner he goes the better.' *Balaam*

The greatest service a parent can render a child is to throw school reports unread into the waste-paper basket.

Robert Morley

FURTHER EDUCATION

I've over-educated myself in all the things I shouldn't have known at all.

Noel Coward

The best pupil I've ever had! I've learnt more modern Greek smut from him than I'd have believed possible.

R. M. Dawkins (Professor of Greek at Oxford)

The average Ph.D thesis is nothing but a transference of bones from one graveyard to another.

J. Frank Dobie

POSH SCHOOLS

Anyone who has been to an English public school will always feel comparatively at home in prison.

Evelyn Waugh

The only saving grace of being at a boarding-school was freedom from my mother's cooking.

Spike Hughes

He can just read and write – Eton, of course.   *Lawrence Durrell*

At English boarding schools, from the ages of nine to eighteen, to be cold was to be manly. Water freezing in wash-basins was very manly.

Arthur Marshall

Educated during the holidays from Eton.   *Osbert Sitwell*

After the average public school the remainder of one's life, however unpleasant, cannot fail to seem something of a holiday.

Osbert Sitwell

I had the choice between St Paul's and Westminster Schools. The former wore straw hats, like Harold Lloyd; the latter, top hats, like Fred Astaire . . . I opted for Westminster.

Peter Ustinov

SIXTH-FORM PRIVILEGE

Loaded firearms were strictly forbidden at St Trinian's to all but **Sixth Formers.**   *Timothy Shy*

Egotism

In front of strangers I am smart, talkative, and utterly, utterly charming.

Virginia Graham

Children, not having yet learnt how to be hypocritical, are quite frank about pointing out their own merits.

Virginia Graham

He fell in love with himself at first sight.　　*Anthony Powell*

If other people are going to talk, conversation becomes impossible.

J. M. Whistler

I never loved another person the way I loved myself.　*Mae West*

To love oneself is the beginning of a lifelong romance.

Oscar Wilde

Embarrassment

'Have you ever had the feeling that you'd like to get inside your handbag and close it firmly above your head?'

Michael Frayn

It left me feeling like something the cat had brought in, and not a very discriminating cat at that.

P. G. Wodehouse

Emotion

The head never rules the heart but just becomes its partner in crime.

Mignon McLaughlin

Enemies

Clark Gable has enemies all right – but they all like him!

David Selznick

Hatred is the coward's revenge for being intimidated.

George Bernard Shaw

Ashes to ashes, and clay to clay,
If the enemy don't get you your own folks may.

James Thurber

The English

It is the perpetual boast of the Englishman that he never brags.
Wyndham Lewis

'We were not fairly beaten. No Englishman is ever fairly beaten.'
George Bernard Shaw

The English would believe anything as long as it wasn't the truth.
E. Somerville and Martin Ross

Here, thriving in all their rampant glory, are some of the finest
flowerings of the English way of life – foul language, dirty
Wellingtons, wife-swapping, and after-hours drinking.
Peter Tinniswood

As a unique courtesy to foreigners, the entire population of the
British Isles deliberately goes to work later than any other in the
world, so as not to disturb tourists.
Barry Humphries

NORTH AND SOUTH

Only Northerners are permitted to be trade union leaders or
comedians.
Oliver Pritchett

In a few years' time the South of England will be buried under an
immense slag-heap consisting of all the earth dug out of the
ground to build the Channel Tunnel and its approaches.
Oliver Pritchett

THE ENGLISH AT TABLE

My wife is now secretly educating the English; they do not really
mind good food as long as the improvement is gradual.
Duke of Bedford

The English became so passionately fond of vinegar that they can
only just be restrained from pouring it into their tea.
Spike Hughes

Coffee in England always tastes like a chemistry experiment.
Agatha Christie

Epitaphs

Dread Death alone could place embargo
Upon the tongue and pen of Margot. (Lady Asquith)
Kensal Green

God found the universe
Going from bad to worse,
So He said, 'Send for Mr Wells . . .'
Wells said, though looking glum,
'Very well; say I'll come.' (H. G. Wells)

Kensall Green

Here lies John Brown, and what is something rarish,
He was born, bred, and hanged, all in the same parish.

Anon

Etiquette

All my mother did until she married was to drive round with my grandmother dropping cards on people who were out dropping cards on her.

Virginia Graham

Faces

I have no doubt whatever that the first joke dealt with the face of the other person involved.

E. V. Lucas

He had a soup-strainer moustache capable of arresting even unfilterable microbes.

F. E. Baily

He had a pair of outsize ears which attracted flies.

Spike Milligan

Even in his twenties George Sanders had a face which looked as though he had rented it on a long lease.

David Niven

I'm not a dictator. It's just that I have a grumpy face.

General Pinochet (Chile)

Eric [Morecambe] has made his way through life trading on the popular belief that toughies won't hit a bloke wearing glasses.

Ernie Wise

Fame

A celebrity is a person who works hard to become well-known, and then wears dark glasses to avoid being recognized.

Fred Allen

There is a lot to be said for not being known to the readers of the *Daily Mirror*.

Anthony Burgess

Fame is the straightforward arithmetical business of being known to more people than you know.

Jonathan Miller

Family

One year I bought the wife's mother a fireside chair. It cost a lot of money. That's why I was annoyed that it fused when I plugged it in.

Les Dawson

No member of the family ever interferes with another except when he thinks the other member is doing something wrong – which is most of the time.

Gerald Durrell

If you cannot get rid of the family skeleton, you may as well make it dance.

George Bernard Shaw

Farming

Farming looks mighty easy when your plough is just a pencil.

Dwight D. Eisenhower

The farmer will never be happy again;
    He carries his heart in his boots;
For either the rain is destroying his grain
    Or the drought is destroying his roots.   *A. P. Herbert*

Last year we farmed on faith; this year we farmed on hope; and next we shall farm on charity.

Anon

Flattery

If you want to win affection and respect, compliment everybody upon everything, and especially upon what they haven't got.

J. K. Jerome

Immigration is the sincerest form of flattery.   *Denis Norden*

What really flatters a man is that you think him worth flattering.

George Bernard Shaw

Flight

The distances passengers have to march through airport terminals is designed to ensure that when you climb into the aircraft you are so exhausted that you fall asleep instantly.   *Prince Charles*

Once inside the terminal (sinister word) you will find a board on which all flights but the one you are hoping to meet are listed.
Robert Morley

Airline travel is hours of boredom interrupted by moments of stark terror.
Al Boliska

Flowers

People here [America] value flowers as sex-cum-affluence tokens and send . . . orchids [to girls] they would barely recognize.
Kingsley Amis

I don't mind what the flowers do in the privacy of their own flowerbeds, or even vases, so long as they don't frighten the bumble-bees.
Barry Humphries

A rose by any other name would be just as expensive.
Lambert Jeffries

Why is it no one ever sent me yet
    One perfect limousine, do you suppose?
Ah no, it's always just my luck to get
    One perfect rose.   *Dorothy Parker*

Food

BAD FOOD GUIDE

Chop: piece of leather skilfully attached to a bone and administered to the patients at restaurants.
Custard: a detestable substance produced by a malevolent conspiracy of the hen, the cow, and the cook.
Ambrose Bierce

He had always been unbalanced. He liked custard poured over his prunes.
Lawrence Durrell

A man appeared in court at Wakefield wearing overalls provided by the police. While in the cells he had eaten his own trousers.
Daily Telegraph

Those pock-marked wafers known as Swedish bread, which produce so cheerless an impression of Scandinavian home life.

Peter Fleming

The roast beef was grey and dessicated, and covered with gravy apparently made from brown boot polish.

Richard Gordon

To duplicate the taste of hammer-head shark, boil old newspapers in Sloan's Liniment.

Spike Milligan

Muesli always looks like the sweepings from a better-class stable.

Frank Muir

Party will leave bus station and alight at Highcliffe. Tea at Barton-on-Sea. Small chisels advised.

(Natural Science Society programme)

Everything I eat has been proved by some doctor or other to be poison.

George Bernard Shaw

GOURMETS

The only thing that tastes exactly like butter is butter.

Arthur Marshall

Seated at table with Red Skelton, I alerted him to the effect that a caterpillar was roaming around in his salad. 'Hmmm . . . nice,' said Red, and ate it.

David Niven

More people will come to visit your stately home because of your good steaks than because of your good Velázquezes.

Duke of Bedford

As a child I helped to make the cakes by stoning the raisins – and eating them.

Dylan Thomas

PUTTING ON WEIGHT

Edward VII and his cronies went in for twenty-four courses, with a sorbet in the middle to let them get their second wind.

Maurice Richardson

Overeating is the most worthy of sins. It neither breaks up marriages nor causes road accidents.

Richard Gordon

Food is a dangerous article. Too much food makes you fat, too little food makes you dead.

Mike Harding

There is no love sincerer than the love of food.

George Bernard Shaw

FAST FOOD

Man could live on tinned soup alone. It heats up in a jiffy, and, more than that, the tin can be used as a throwaway saucepan.

Frank Muir

After Royal Garden Parties, gardeners frequently find merinques with false teeth stuck in them, where they have been hurriedly disposed of behind a bush at the approach of Her Majesty.

Douglas Sutherland

Football

The woman sits, getting colder and colder, on a seat getting harder and harder, watching oafs getting muddier and muddier.

Virginia Graham

The holy writ of Gloucester Rugby club demands, first, that the forwards shall win the ball, second, that the forwards shall keep the ball, and third, that the backs shall buy the beer.

Doug Ibbotson

The practice of footballers kissing each other after a goal is scored has lowered the tone.

Douglas Sutherland

I would have thought that the knowledge that you are going to be leapt upon by half-a-dozen congratulatory but sweaty team-mates would be an inducement *not* to score a goal at Soccer.

Arthur Marshall

In my time I've had my knee put out, broken my collar-bone, had my nose smashed, a rib broken, lost a few teeth, and ricked my ankle, but as soon as I get a bit of bad luck I'm going to quit the game.

J. W. Robinson

Foreigners

There comes a dreadful moment in our lives when foreign friends, whom we strongly urged to visit us, actually do so.

Virginia Graham

I can't see that foreign stories are ever news – not *real* news.

Evelyn Waugh

France

Famed as the French always are for ragouts,
No creature can tell what they put in their stews,
Whether bull-frogs, old gloves, or old wigs, or old shoes.

R. H. Barham

A truthful man told me that the French buy less soap than any
other nation west of the Iron Curtain.

Tom Sharpe

It's strange the French prove, when they take to aspersing,
So inferior to us in the science of cursing.

R. H. Barham

Chacon à son goût – everybody has gout sooner or later.

Harry Graham

In Boulogne the children went off to select French souvenirs. They
came back with Dinky cars, made in England.

Tina Spencer Knott

Friendship

Love thy neighbour as thyself – but choose your neighbourhood.

Louise Beal

The great thing about Errol Flynn was – you always knew
precisely where you stood with him because he *always* let you
down.

David Niven

You can tell the person who lives for others by the haunted look
on the faces of the others.

Katherine Whitehorn

One's friends, as a class, are able to view one's misfortunes with
fortitude.

P. G. Wodehouse

Frustration

When things just can't get any worse, they will. (*Chisholm's Law*)

If you're looking for something in a hurry you won't find it, even if
it is staring you in the face.

Lambert Jeffries

The easiest way to find something you've lost is to buy a
replacement.

Leonard Rossiter

If you get rid of something, you will want it the following day.

Lambert Jeffries

My glasses are very evasive. When I'm upstairs they're always downstairs, and vice versa; and when I'm in the bedroom they're bound to be in the bathroom, with the door locked.

Lambert Jeffries

It seems to be the rule that each person has what he doesn't want, and other people have what he does want.

J. K. Jerome

If you just tear casually at a sheet of stamps, it tears across the Queen's head.

Miles Kington

Any wire cut exactly to length will be too short. *(Klipstein's Law)*

Future

That period of time in which our affairs prosper, our friends are true, and our happiness is assured.

Ambrose Bierce

The future is something which everyone reaches at the rate of sixty mintues an hour.

C. S. Lewis

The only thing to be said in favour of the future is that we don't, thank God, know what's coming our way.

Arthur Marshall

Time enough to think of the future when you haven't any future to think of.

George Bernard Shaw

Gardeners' World

She has experimented with playing a recording of a male voice choir to cucumbers.

Daily Telegraph

My favourite area in the garden is the compost heap.

James Reeve (artist)

Whoever heard of a serious crime being committed by a gardener?

Harry Graham

It is forbidden to be half-hearted about gardening. You have got to *love* your garden, whether you like it or not.

W. C. Sellar and R. J. Yeatman

It was one of those glorious May days when motor-mowers chatter happily to each other across back fences.

Richard Gordon

PROBLEMS AND PESTS

'Normal' pruning weather is always bitterly cold with the wind in the north-east.

Spike Hughes

Armies of slugs have embarked, without formal declaration, on what has proved to be the opening campaign of another Hundred Years War.

Spike Hughes

Slugs nearly always share the tastes of those in whose gardens they live.

Spike Hughes

Weeds are deep-thinking organisms, and to keep worrying them only produces a profound sense of bitterness which drives them into all kinds of displeasing subterfuges.

Eric Keown

If you are giving your plants food, stop. If you are not feeding them, start immediately. This is based on the theory that whatever you are doing, it is bound to be wrong.

Miles Kington

THE ART OF TOOL-LENDING

He asked whether he could borrow my lawn-mower. I said, 'Of course you can, so long as you don't take it out of my garden.'

Eric Morecambe

GRIM GARDENING

Gardening is a high risk occupation . . . when the fork has impaled your foot, the scythe cut you to the bone, the grass-cutter electrocuted you, and the bonfire burnt down the house.

Robert Morley

A garden is a loathsome thing, God wot,
Weeds flourish, things that you plant do not.

Lambert Jeffries

Golf

Any golfer whose ball hits a seagull shall be said to have scored a 'birdie'.

Frank Muir

You hit the ball, and if it doesn't go far enough you just hit it again, and if that doesn't work you hit it again, and so on.

Robert Robinson

You can't play a really hot game unless you're so miserable that you don't worry over your shots.

P. G. Wodehouse

Graffiti

Reality is an illusion caused by lack of alcohol.

Absinthe makes the tart grow fonder.

Be unselfish. Give up what you don't want.

Blacks unite! Down with racism!

Don't bother to think ahead. Tomorrow will soon be yesterday.

God is not dead. He's merely working on a less ambitious project.

If you want a light meal try eating a candle.

I'm a Marxist. Good old Groucho!

I don't want to buy pornographic pictures. I don't even own a pornograph.

Laugh and the world laughs with you. Silly sheep!

Let the people sing! They can't be worse than pop singers.

Owing to lack of interest, tomorrow has been cancelled.

Pick your own strawberries – ready for the next traffic jam.

So there's a population explosion? But it's fun helping to light the fuse.

We didn't invent sin. We're just trying to improve it.

What's afoot? The thing attached to your ankle.

Why does a giraffe have a long neck? Because it doesn't like the smell of its feet.

Death is life's answer to 'Why?'

Goodness

A good deed never goes unpunished.

Oscar Wilde

Hair

Did you know that there are 100,000 hairs on the average scalp? Using your thumb and forefinger, see if you can discover how you compare with the average.

Barry Humphries

A thin long-nosed woman . . . with a very short hair-do, which gave her head and neck a melancholy, denuded appearance, like a tree cut back for the winter.

Kingsley Amis

A barber's shop in Doha, in the Gulf-state of Qatar, sports the sign: 'Hair-cutting while you wait'.

The Daily Telegraph

I view with deep suspicion any man who actually looks forward to going to the hairdresser.

Beryl Downing

A Cockney kid, staring through the window of a barber's shop while a customer was having his hair singed, exclaimed: 'Blimey, he's looking for 'em wiv a light!'

Lord Hill of Luton

A CHANGE OF HAIR

I darkened my hair to show that I have character and brains.

Angela Joyce (former Beauty Queen)

'I used to be angry with my young son for constantly slapping my bald pate. But I changed my view when I found my hair starting to grow again.'

Tit-Bits (letter)

I hear her hair has turned quite gold from grief.   *Oscar Wilde*

Happiness

I have been happy all my life . . . It results from a combination of heredity, health, good fortune, and shallow intellect.

Arthur Marshall

History

Think of Magna Carta! Did she die in vain?   *Tony Hancock*

Although God cannot alter the past, historians can.
Samuel Butler

I have seen men trying to teach history who hardly knew whether the Armada was a town in Brazil or a winner of the Derby.
Balaam

History repeats itself. Historians repeat each other.
Philip Guedalla

Red-haired people are poor at history, according to an Oxford history examiner.
This England

Holidays

To return from holiday without a bronzed skin is as humiliating as Jason coming home without the Golden Fleece.
Richard Gordon

Most holiday returnees tell the tale of the train that broke down, the traffic that jammed, the sunburn that peeled off painfully.
Paul Barker

A new German phrasebook starts its section 'Enjoying Your Stay' with some handy expressions such as: 'I cannot turn the heating off; the lock is broken; there is no plug in the wash-basin; there is no toilet paper.'
Daily Telegraph

Our holiday at Blackpool was ruined by canoodling couples . . . For our next holiday we shall go to Bournemouth.
Empire News

When you reach your destination you will queue up twelve times a day: three times for ice-cream, twice for deck-chairs, three times for beer, once for tea, twice for swings for the children, and once for the hell of it.
George Mikes

THE ENGLISHMAN ABROAD

You will feel much more tranquil abroad if you bring along some comfortable object long familiar at home. Your spouse, for example.
Richard Gordon

The Londoner abroad, the cautious chap,
Dares not to drink from any foreign tap.   *A. P. Herbert*

We can generally make ourselves understood abroad by shouting each word slowly and clearly, and beating time on a convenient piece of furniture with an umbrella.

Edward Leslie

Home

I've been away only five days, yet the cobwebs look as though they've been there for years.

Beata Bishop

Take your old sheets and cut them up for dust covers; you want to keep your dust looking nice.

Peg Bracken

To house agents, 'utility room' means a room too small to get a bed in. 'Secluded' means completely cut off from all light by surrounding high-rise flats and blank wall facing kitchen window.

Derek Cooper

Always clean the inside of your windows. Then you'll be able to see outside but the neighbours won't be able to see inside.

George Formby Jnr

Why is it, as soon as you've poured the washing-up water away, a dirty cup is always found hiding behind an armchair?

Lambert Jeffries

I want a house that has got over all its troubles; I don't want to spend the rest of my life bringing up a young and inexperienced house.

J. K. Jerome

To grow rosemary outside the front door means that the woman rules the house.

Spike Hughes

I shouldn't have been in the morning-room because it was half-past two in the afternoon, but I couldn't go into the sitting-room because I wanted to stand.

Frank Muir

Horses

He didn't really ride; he conned horses into letting him sit on them.   *David Niven*

Any money I put on a horse is a sort of insurance policy to prevent it winning.

Frank Richardson

While horses are walking you can't tell the difference between me and Nimrod: it's when they start going a bit faster that the fraudulence of my boots and breeches becomes apparent.

Robert Robinson

Nobody has any right to go around looking like a horse.

Dorothy Parker

I backed the right horse but the wrong horse went and won.

Henry Arthur Jones and Henry Herman

'You may have my husband but not my horse.'   *D. H. Lawrence*

GUIDE TO THE TURF

At a time when Edgar Wallace was losing £100 a day at the races the *Evening Standard* engaged him as a racing tipster.

Derek Cooper

Remember – Lady Godiva put everything she had on a horse.

W. C. Fields

In most betting shops you will see three windows marked Bet Here, but only one window with the legend Pay Out.

Jeffrey Barnard

You never see a pretty unattached girl on a racecourse. But you often see positive gangs of rather unpretty ones. They are owners or owners' wives.

Jeffrey Barnard

Hospital

After seeing Madeleine Carroll in *Vigil in the Night* I decided I was going to be a nurse in a pure white halo cap, and glide swiftly about with oxygen cylinders and, if necessary, give my life for a patient.

Monica Dickens

In a fashionable nursing-home he was privileged to occupy a small attic bedroom on the sixth floor, and to enjoy a bill of fare consisting chiefly of underdone plaice and tapioca pudding.

Harry Graham

The biggest gaffe on radio was perhaps by the disc jockey who dedicated a record to everyone in hospital. The record he played was 'When I'm Dead and Gone'.

David Hamilton

Externally the design is modern; internally the treatment is severe, as is usual in a hospital.

Daily Telegraph

Hotels

The [sulphur] smell was vaguely reminiscent of an obscure English railway hotel at lunch-time.

Gerald Durrell

I feel his books are all written in hotels, with the bed unmade.

Ronald Firbank

There's nothing like a few days' residence in a small hotel behind the British Museum for inducing a mood of melancholy introspection.

Richard Gordon

Howlers

Mr Salteena sat down and ate the egg which Ethel had so kindly laid for him.

Daisy Ashford

'St Paul's Cathedral was designed by Sir Christopher Robin.'

Daily Telegraph (quoting)

On the outline map of England and Wales provided, shade in the Highlands of Scotland.

(Lancashire and Cheshire schools examination question)

'The early Britons made their houses of mud, and there was rough mating on the floor.'

Frank Muir (quoting)

It was so still you could have picked up a pin.

Linley Sambourne (former *Punch* artist)

Sir Francis Drake said, 'The Armada can wait but my bowels can't'.

Anon

Thomas Hardy wrote *Tess of the Dormobiles*.

Anon

Bach wrote many tunes and had many children, and in between he practised on a spinster in the attic.

Anon

Socrates died from an overdose of wedlock.

Anon

The French National Anthem is the *Mayonnaise*.

Anon

The Royal Navy is sometimes called the senile service.

Anon

Humour

Most of the time I don't have much fun. The rest of the time I don't have any fun at all.

Woody Allen

If not the best of all possible worlds, this is certainly the most amusing.

William Archer

I can't help laughing. I know what's coming.　*Tommy Cooper*

The essence of humour is surprise; that is why you laugh when you see a joke in *Punch*.

A. P. Herbert

'He's got no sense of humour. If he fell out of bed and cut himself on a tooth-glass, he wouldn't laugh.'

W. Douglas Home

JOKES

The jokes have been purloined from old W. C. Fields routines, Bob Hope films, obscure vaudeville acts, and discarded Christmas crackers.

Peter Jackson

Although nobody has ever seen anyone fall over on a banana skin, this has for some reason been elected as the prime example of a joke.

Miles Kington

Peter Ustinov once imitated a German telling a joke: 'First I will tell you about the joke I am about to tell you. Then I will tell the joke; after which I will exlain it, and then you may laugh.'

Miles Kington

A new joke is one you have never heard before. An old joke is one you've heard once.

Myles Palmer

Huntin' and Shootin'

An important reason for retaining bright coats in the hunting field is that the wearing of them signifies a feeling of respect towards the farmers over whose land the hunt rides.

Farmer & Stock-Breeder

Deer-stalking would be very fine sport if only the deer had guns.

W. S. Gilbert

I have known a fox that was absolutely devoted to fox-hunting.
Colonel Sir Lancelot Rolleston MFH

The keeping down of foxes is felt by most gentlemen to be part of the responsibility of their station in life, even if it means making sure that there is always a sufficiently supply of foxes to be kept down.
Douglas Sutherland

'Of course I didn't keep looking to see if my stole was still there. I would at an ordinary dance, but this was a hunt ball!'
Sunday Express

Husbands and Wives

Being pregnant . . . is an occupational hazard of being a wife.
Princess Anne

You can't expect to take a wife shopping and just come out with what you went in for.
J. B. Boothroyd

For our auction we would be grateful for anything you want to get rid of. Come on the day and bring your husbands.
(Women's Institute notice)

Why are they always called wife-swapping parties, never husband-swapping parties?
Peg Bracken

If you want to pull wool over your wife's eyes, you need to have a good yarn.
Gyles Brandreth

The reason that husbands and wives don't understand each other is because they belong to different sexes.
Dorothy Dix

Zsa Zsa Gabor once told me that she and Conrad Hilton, her millionaire ex-husband, only had one thing in common – *his* money.
David Niven

'I shall see in the greasy eyes of all the other husbands their relief at the arrival of a new prisoner to share their ignominy.'
George Bernard Shaw

Mr Glynn Wolfe of Los Angeles, the world's most married man, has just left his 26th wife. 'One of these days I'm going to find the right woman,' he said.
Sunday Telegraph

Christians are only allowed one wife and this is is known as monotony.
(Anonymous schoolboy)

Illness

I've just learnt about his illness; let's hope it's nothing trivial.

Irvin Cobb

There never was such a boy for getting ill. He would go out in a November fog and come home with sunstroke.

J. K. Jerome

KEEP TAKING THE TABLETS

'My whole mentality is geared to swallowing tablets every three hours, 24 hours a day.'

Alan Ayckbourn

'I've just taken fifty sleeping pills. The pink ones.'
'Those aren't sleeping pills. They're laxatives.'

Alan Bennett

REMEDIAL TREATMENT

An aching head soon makes one forget an aching heart.

J. K. Jerome

There's nothing the matter with being sick that getting well can't fix.

Peg Bracken

Whisky is the most popular of all the cold cures that don't work.

Leonard Rossiter

If you take suitable medicine for a cold it will clear up in seven days. If you leave the cold to cure itself it will take a week.

Anon

We had to give him the kiss of life with a bicycle pump.

Lawrence Durrell

'I get through first-aid tins like loaves of bread.'

Alan Ayckbourn

LOSING BATTLE

As soon as the doctors are able to pronounce that a particularly deadly disease can be cured, Nature provides another one.

Henry Cecil

Most people over the age of fifty have rheumatism, and it is impossible to make it much better or much worse with any form of treatment.

Richard Gordon

HOSPITAL TREATMENT

Sir Arbuthnot Lane of Guy's Hospital was mad on constipation. He made a fortune by filling his patients with liquid paraffin until they leaked like coach-lamps.

Richard Gordon

I was at an RAF hospital in the country being treated for shock – brought on by the realisation that I was about to be demobilised and would have to work for a living.

Denis Norden

When they knock on my nursing home door, I say, 'Who goes there? Friend or enema?'

Eric Morecambe

Insults
INSULTS OFF THE CUFF

'You total and utter grubby, smutty, grimy, unhygienic little bitch!'

Alan Ayckbourn

'Have you ever thought of having a brain transplant?'

Michael Frayn

The judge summed up like a drunken monkey.   *W. S. Gilbert*

You fat, stupid, loud-mouthed, thick-skinned, ill-mannered creep.

Alfred Grossman

I wish I'd known you when you were alive.   *L. L. Levinson*

Had your father spent more of your mother's immoral earnings on your education you would not even then have been a gentleman.

Frank Otter

'You're looking nicer than usual,' I said, 'but that's so easy for you.'   *Saki*

You have a head, and so has a pin.   *Jonathan Swift*

If only he'd wash his neck I'd wring it.   *John Sparrow*

You're a big existential garbage-pail.   *Anon*

PREMEDITATED INSULTS

George the Third
Ought never to have occurred.
One can only wonder
At so grotesque a blunder.

E. C. Bentley

A deadly winking, sniggering, snuggling, chromium-plated, scent-impregnated, luminous, quivering, giggling, mincing, heap of mother love.

William Connor (on Liberace)

The psychiatrist . . . had the eye and warmth of a dead trout.

Richard Gordon

He is a slimy, slinking, marcelle-waved . . . snake in the grass, a pestilence, a pustule, a blister.

Geoffrey Jaggard

There's so much wool in his head it's easy to pull it over his eyes.

Anthony Jay and Jonathan Lynn

The jelly-boned swine, the slimy, the belly-wriggling invertebrates, the miserable sodding rotters, the flaming sods, the snivelling, dribbling, dithering, palsied, pulseless lot that make up England today.

D. H. Lawrence (on the fellow-countrymen who failed to appreciate his work)

Nothing but old fags and cabbage stumps . . . stewed in the juice of deliberate journalistic dirty-mindedness.

D. H. Lawrence (on James Joyce)

A cigar-smoking, stale-aired, slack-jawed, butt-littered, foul . . . death gas of language and faces.

Norman Mailer (on a Democratic National Convention)

Yellow teeth protruded from beneath a small nicotine-stained moustache, and a receding chin did nothing to help a pair of shifty eyes that were pinned together like cuff-links above a beaky nose.

David Niven

To me, Edith looks like something that would eat its young.

Dorothy Parker

'When your inclusion in the house-party was suggested, Sir Wilfred protested that there was a wide distinction between hospitality and the care of the feeble-minded.'

Saki

'That trunk of humours, that bolting-hutch of beastliness, that swoln parcel of dropsies, that huge bombard of sack, that stuffed cloak-bag of guts.'

William Shakespeare (Falstaff)

A gap-toothed and hoary-headed ape . . . who now in his dotage spits and chatters from a dirtier perch of his own finding and fouling.

A. C. Swinburne (on R. W. Emerson)

She's had eleven husbands – including three of her own.   *Anon*

Ireland

The Irish are a fair people. They never speak well of one another.
Samuel Johnson

If it was raining soup, we'd be out with forks. *Brendan Behan*

The quiet Irishman is about as harmless as a powder magazine built over a match factory.
James Dunne

He was a sort of Irish/Jewish gnome – so they called him a lepra-Cohen.
Kevin Goldstein-Jackson

Irishwoman to Irishman: 'I've set the alarm clock for six.' 'Why? there's only two of us.'
Spike Milligan

The Irish don't want anyone to wish them well; they want them to wish their enemies ill.
Harold Nicholson

'You were supposed to call to mend my doorbell yesterday. Why didn't you come?'
'Begorra, I did so, I rang but I couldn't get an answer.' *Anon*

Irreligion

Irreligion is one of the great faiths of the world. *Ambrose Bierce*

She believed in nothing; only her scepticism kept her from being an atheist.
Jean-Paul Sartre

Journalists

When you hear something described by a journalist as disturbing, you know you cannot take it seriously.
Kenneth Robinson

An investigating journalist is one who can think up plausible scandals.
Lambert Jeffries

One of my prize dropped bricks occurred when I was interviewing the wife of the Swedish ambassador about how much entertaining had to be done. 'Tell me,' I asked, 'does your husband have big balls?'
Lynne Reid Banks

A Fleet Street editor exhorted his staff to shun clichés like the plague. *Peter Durrant*

You cannot hope to bribe or twist
Thank God! the British journalist.
But seeing what the man will do
Unbribed, there's no occasion to. *Humbert Wolfe*

WHAT THE PAPERS SAY

Good news is no news. *Lambert Jeffries*

Journalism largely consists in saying 'Lord Jones Dead' to people who never knew Lord Jones was alive.
G. K. Chesterton

News is what a chap who doesn't care much about anything wants to read.
Evelyn Waugh

We never check our stories. If you check them they often turn out not to be true. (Anonymous journalist)

It is better to dip into *The Last Days of Pompeii* at breakfast than to peruse the morning paper.
James Thurber

In the columns of the *Staffordshire Signal* burglars never get into a residence; they effect an entrance.
Arnold Bennett

READERS

She will take in the *New Statesman,* but she won't be taken in.
Joyce Grenfell

All the way down in the train I read the newspaper upside down, and never enjoyed it so much. It's really the only way to read newspapers.
Oscar Wilde

'We hardly know each other, yet I have been selected from so many millions to enter your free contest in which I may win £25,000 . . . You have made me very happy.'
Miles Kington (to *Reader's Digest*)

Anyone who is rung up by more than one reporter thinks he's being hounded.
Woodrow Wyatt

PASSING THOUGHT

Whole forests are being ground into pulp daily to minister to our triviality. *Irving Babbitt*

Kissing

A kiss that speaks volumes is seldom a first edition. *Clare Whiting*

He groped his way blindly through a phalanx of lovers, with kisses popping like champagne corks on every side.

Eric Barker

There was a beautiful statue of Cupid and Psyche kissing. Wordsworth's face reddened, and he said in a loud voice, 'The Dev-v-vils!'

Benjamin Haydon

The sound of a kiss is not as loud as that of a cannon, but its echo lasts longer.

O. W. Holmes

Mayhem, death, and arson
Have followed many a thoughtless kiss
Not sanctioned by a parson.   *Don Marquis*

She's the type who kisses hello and shakes hands good-night.

Reader's Digest

I spend most of my time kissing people on the cheek in order to get them to do what they ought to do without being kissed.

Harry Truman

Georgie Porgie pudding and pie
Kissed the girls and made them cry;
When the boys came out to play
He kissed them too, he's funny that way.   *Anon*

Language

In Paris I never succeeded in making those idiots understand their own language.

Mark Twain

I acquired such skill in reading Latin and Greek that I could take a page of either, and distinguish which language it was by merely glancing at it.

Stephen Leacock

To 'language up' an opponent is . . . 'to confuse, irritate and depress by the use of foreign words, fictitious or otherwise'.

Stephen Potter

A gifted person ought to learn English in thirty hours, French in thirty days, and German in thirty years.

Mark Twain

I don't mind what language an opera is sung in so long as it's a language I don't understand.

Edward Appleton

Lawyers

Lawyer: one skilled in circumvention of the law. *Ambrose Bierce*

There had been a fellow in prison whose lawyer was later known to boast that he had got him a suspended sentence. They hanged him.

Brendan Behan

If we lawyers only took cases in which we really believed we'd go out of business in no time.

Henry Cecil

A law bookshop . . . had spent years piling incomprehensible jargon on to its shelves so that the legal profession could keep the layman at bay and the wolf from the door.

Alan Coren

An appeal is when you ask one court to show its contempt for another court.

Finley Peter Dunne

A jury consists of twelve persons chosen to decide who has the better lawyer.

Robert Frost

If it weren't for insurance companies there would be little litigation.

A. P. Herbert

LAYMEN

The jury were twelve honest, understanding British citizens who had all previously written notes explaining that they would be unable to do jury service because of bilious attacks, nosebleeds, dying relatives, flat feet . . . and religious holidays.

Alan Coren

An Act of God was defined as 'something which no reasonable man could have expected'.

A. P. Herbert

Lawyers have a favourite expression: 'He lies like an eyewitness'.

Don Murray

They say in law that there is no such thing as a Reasonable Woman. There is no such thing in life, I think, as a reasonable anybody.

Katherine Whitehorn

If you can understand a contract, it must be legally unsound.

Lambert Jeffries

Letters

You don't know a woman until you have had a letter from her.

Ada Leverson

The very thought of letter-writing can turn one's brain into something resembling cold porridge.

Christopher Matthew

The notepaper of the late Penelope Betjeman used to say, 'No telephone – thank God'.

Mark Steyn

Nothing so lifts a soldier's morale as getting a letter from home, and nothing so depresses him as reading it.

Thornton Wilder

Life

Isn't life a terrible thing, thank God. *Dylan Thomas*

I've crashed through life dropping bricks upon every corn in sight.

John Braine

Life was a damned muddle . . . a football game with everyone offside.

F. Scott Fitzgerald

Isn't your life extremely flat
With nothing whatever to grumble at.

W. S. Gilbert

You should go on living just to annoy those who are paying your annuities.

Voltaire

Life is a table d'hôte meal, with Time changing the plates before you've had enough of anything.

Thomas Kettle

We discovered early in life that to go on living was the only way to survive.

Groucho Marx

It's not true that Life is one damn thing after another – it's one damn thing over and over.

Edna St Vincent Millay

Life is the best teacher of all, though the fees on occasion come somewhat expensive.

Richard Gordon

LOOKING AT LIFE

I would enjoy the day more if it started later. *(Graffito)*

It is when all is apparently well with your world that Fate so often plants a length of lead piping across the base of the cranium.

Geoffrey Green

It's a mad world, isn't it? And I can never quite decide which side of the asylum wall is the inside.

W. Douglas Home

My sole is crushed, my spirit sore,
I do not like me any more.

Dorothy Parker

The race is not always to the swift nor the battle to the strong, but that's the way to bet.

Damon Runyon

Put all your eggs in one basket – and watch the basket.

Mark Twain

Literature

Carlyle's *Sartor Resartus* is quite unreadable, and to me that always sort of spoils a book.

Will Cuppy

Oscar was Wilde but Thornton was even Wilder. *(Graffito)*

To the colleges Milton seems profound because he wrote of Hell, an important place, and is dead.

Stephen Leacock

A classic is something that everybody wants to have read and nobody wants to read.

Mark Twain

The Nobel Prize for Literature, judged by a committee of humourless Swedes, might as well be awarded on the tombola principle.

Auberon Waugh

The difference between journalism and literature is that journalism is unreadable and literature is not read.

Oscar Wilde

A man would need a heart of stone not to laugh at the death of Little Nell

Oscar Wilde

London

London is chaos incorporated.

George Mikes

At the Tower, unfortunately, beheadings have become rather few and far between, and are not included in the entrance fee.

Duke of Bedford and George Mikes

Buckingham Palace, the Queen's delightful home in the London suburb of Westminster.

Barry Humphries

The notion that in the London winter people never see the sun is, of course, a ridiculous error . . . I have myself plainly seen it on a November day in broad daylight.

Stephen Leacock

Loos

Why does the telephone always ring when you're in the loo and there's no one else to answer it?

Lambert Jeffries

There is a regrettable lack of essential stationery in the visitors' bathroom.

Hester Alington (wife of Eton headmaster)

When opening a stately home . . . the very first thing you need is good loos.

Duke of Bedford and George Mikes

A Methodist minister's acts of gross indecency in a public lavatory might eventually 'enrich his ministry', Lord Soper told the Court.

Daily Telegraph

Because most of the immigrants aboard ship could not read, the Ladies' lavatory was normally infested with males who proceeded to remove all the seats.

Jacquie Durrell

A meeting at Saxmundham . . . decided that a memorial for King George VI should take the form of a public convenience.

East Anglian Daily Times

At last! – a warm toilet seat. Like sitting on toast (Advertisement.) Let's hope, for everyone's sake, it's not one of those that pops up.

Frank Muir

You never realize how much furniture you've collected till you have to go to the loo in the dark.

Denis Norden

When the First World War broke out she took down the signed photograph of the Kaiser . . . and hung it in the menservants' lavatory.

Evelyn Waugh

At Swindon, new public lavatories have the outside railings painted pink for women and blue for men. A Labour councillor complains that this is sexist.

(Newspaper report)

When he goes to the toilet, to save embarrassment he gives a cough to let the neighbours above and below know he is there.

Richmond and Twickenham Times

Love

He folded her in his arms, using the interlocking grip.

P. G. Wodehouse

My new fiancé, Denzil here,
Is keen on heavy petting;
He wants to go too far with me
And by God I'm going to let him.

Alan Bennett

One man's mate is another man's poison.   *Richard Gordon*

Nearly all soul-mates find each other in the end by trial and error, and the more trial the less error.

A. P. Herbert

Fancy a man trying to make love on strictly truthful principles!

J. K. Jerome

I find on looking back in my diaries that I always fall in love on Thursdays. Is there any reason why this should be so? (Letter in daily paper)

This England

LOVE AND MARRIAGE

Love is blind, but marriage restores its sight.   *G. C. Lichtenberg*

Sending your girl's love letters to your rival after he has married her is one form of revenge.

Ambrose Bierce

The trouble with lovers is that most of them have a habit of turning into husbands.

Diana Dors

Machinery

I marched into a lift, pressed the third floor button, and dropped like a stone to the second basement.

J. B. Boothroyd

My electric cooker is a legacy from the house's previous owners. If you turn on all four burners you fuse the whole house – and probably the village.

Edwina Currie

It's amazing how many quick repairs a woman can fix with an ordinary kitchen knife, whereas a man can't lift a finger without his tool-chest.

Tina Spencer Knott

All machines are more wilful than animals – strange, nervous, irritable things.

Oscar Wilde

Magic

Chief among the mysteries of India is how the natives keep those little loin cloths up.

Robert Benchley

Don't plan to earn a living doing magic. If you must live dangerously, become a bank robber, so if you do fail, the government will keep and feed you.

Lou Derman

Fred Kaps performed his famous Floating Cork, and all agreed that it was the best close-up trick invented since sex.

Lou Derman

There was an unfortunate lapse in concentration during his 'Sawing a Woman in Half' illusion. Fortunately the mishap didn't prove fatal, and the lady concerned is now living contentedly in Scarborough. And Devon.

Denis Norden

Man's Best Friend

For many of us, particularly myself, a dog is a set of sharp teeth mounted on four legs.

Robert Morley

Jill's Corgi bit the postman; we had to give the dog away to a woman in Headington, who liked the idea of a dog that bit postmen.

S. P. B. Mais

Dogs, like horses, are quadrupeds. That is to say, they have four rupeds, one at each corner.

Frank Muir

In *Macbeth* a dog misbehaves himself in the castle and Lady Macbeth, very cross, cries 'Out, damned Spot!'

Frank Muir

He was a large dog with a blunt, stupid face, and a faculty for excitement about nothing. Had he been able to speak he would have asked idiotic questions.

E. Somerville and Martin Ross

If you try to beat the blunt end of a terrier you find yourself suddenly assaulted by the sharp end.

John Tickner

Having originated from a Bulldog and Terrier cross, a Bull Terrier can get very cross indeed.

John Tickner

And now, here are the results of the Sheepdog Trials. All the sheepdogs were found Not Guilty.

Keith Waterhouse

If you send your dog to fetch the paper, make sure it knows which one to get, and don't give it too much money or it might not come back.

Mike Harding

Marriage

Marriage is give and take. You'd better give it to her or she'll take it anyway.

Joey Adams

I married beneath me. All women do. *Nancy Astor*

'As far as my husband's concerned, my existence ended on the day he married me. I'm just an embarrassing smudge on a marriage licence.'

Alan Ayckbourn

Every man expects his marriage to be different, and it's a shock to find that it's like everybody else's.

J. B. Boothroyd

It was very good of God to let Carlyle and Mrs Carlyle marry one another and so make only two people miserable instead of four.

Samuel Butler

All comedies are ended by a marriage. *Lord Byron*

FOR BETTER FOR WORSE

A man is incomplete until he's married. Then he's finished.

Zsa Zsa Gabor

Marriage is a lottery, but you can't tear up your ticket if you lose.

F. M. Knowles

Jessica's mother was distressed less by losing a daughter than by the fact that when I knelt at the altar rails she spotted a hole in the sole of one of my shoes.

Jack Hawkins

To stay happily married to anyone for 25 years is an achievement. To stay married for that length of time to a writer is a miracle.

Sheila Hailey (wife of American novelist, *Arthur Hailey*)

'Am I not your wife? Your neglect of me surely proves it.'

John Gay

WHY MARRY?

His designs were strictly honourable . . . that is, to rob a lady of her fortune by way of marriage.

Henry Fielding

The only sort of man most women want to marry is the fella with a will of his own – made out in her favour.

Brendan Behan

I could love you even to matrimony – almost. *John Vanbrugh*

Montezuma, the Aztec king, collected wives the way other men collect hotel towels.

Edward Vernon

'Wilt thou have this woman to thy wedded wife?'
'Oh, decisions, decisions!' *Anon*

A *Which* report in 1983 found that people using dubious match-making agencies had been matched with married men, alcoholics, people living miles away, and even, in one case, with a dead person.

Helen Chappell

MARRIAGE BREAK-UP

Have you ever noticed how people whose marriages are breaking up keep re-decorating the kitchen?

Matthew Parris

I shall marry in haste and repeat at leisure. *James Branch Cabell*

'Three honeymoons, and another in the offing . . . You don't need a marriage licence – what you want is a season ticket!'
W. Douglas Home

Men!

Man was created a little lower than the angels, and has continued getting a little lower ever since.
Josh Billings

Too many tidy females marry men who throw their dirty socks behind the wardrobe.
Beatta Bishop

'Men pick up anything you leave about and clean the car with it.'
J. B. Boothroyd

Men are like fires. If they're not attended to, they go out. *Anon*

Men in fiction attach much more importance to love than do the ordinary men of everyday life.
E. M. Delafield

Only a woman with masochistic tendencies could fall in love with one of those rough, beer-swilling Australian men.
Diana Dors

Rather a man building a motor-cycle in the bedroom than a man twiddling his thumbs in the kitchen.
Virginia Graham

It takes one woman twenty years to make a man of her son, and another woman twenty minutes to make a fool of him.
Helen Rowland

HOW TO HANDLE MEN

No woman should know more than a man. If she wants to be loved, that is.
Virginia Graham

Patience means a willingness to hold the umbrella over his head while he changes a wheel.
Katherine Whitehorn

The hardest task in a girl's life is to prove to a man that his intentions are serious.
Helen Rowland

MEN TO FANCY AND FANCY MEN

I don't think I could ever fancy a man who had to disappear to the men's room to touch up his lipstick.

Diana Dors

I like men to behave like men – strong and childish.

Françoise Sagan

To be able to turn a man out into a garden and tell him to stay there until the next meal, is every woman's dream.

Virginia Graham

He always looks so exceptionally dapper, the local theory is that she keeps a plastic cover over him when not in use.

Denis Norden

MISOGYNISTS

A misogynist is a man who blames women for the lipstick he finds on his glass in a pub, instead of blaming the barman who is supposed to have washed up.

Spike Hughes

MALE READING HABITS

Why is it that there are dozens of heart-throb weeklies for women and none for men?

Tina Spencer Knott

Money

I'm tired of Love; I'm still more tired of Rhyme.
But Money gives me pleasure all the time.

Hilaire Belloc

Being permanently in the red is less alarming than you supposed.

Duke of Bedford

When someone says 'It's the principle of the thing, not the money' – it's the money.

Kin Hubbard

MONEY IN THE BANK

Bankers are just like anybody else, only richer.　　*Ogden Nash*

I've got a lovely wife and family, a dog, and a bank manager to support.

Eric Morecambe

Banks used to frown on you if you tried to spend more than you had. Now they frown on you if you don't.

Lambert Jeffries

THE VALUE OF MONEY

After a school lesson on the value of money a nine-year-old girl stole the money used in the demonstration.

Gloucestershire Echo

I've decided that being poorer than the people you know is a problem. So is being richer.

Peg Bracken

WHO WANTS TO BE A MILLIONAIRE?

Asked if he is a millionaire he replies, 'Yes, but it is rather vulgar to say so'.

Jessica Berens (on Simon Napier-Bell.)

'I did not marry my wife because she had four million. I would have married her even if she had only two million.'

Charles Forte (quoting)

The misery of affluence, which grinds the faces of the rich and forces them to bear the intolerable burden of wealth.

Harry Graham

BILLS, BILLS, BILLS

When the bills come in, there are a number of things you can do besides cry. For one, you can fill in the form for Amount Enclosed . . . and then forget to enclose it.

Peg Bracken

Sometimes I send a cheque and forget to sign it. Sometimes I put the date a year ahead. Sometimes I put one thing in the figures and another in the words.

Henry Cecil

In the midst of life we are in debt.

Ethel Mumford

INSURANCE COVER

There is nearly always a clause in an insurance policy that lets the company out.

S. P. B. Mais

There is simply no way an insurance company can defraud you. All that happened was you didn't read the small print.

Robert Morley

Music

THE SOUND OF MUSIC

Wagner wrote music which is better than it sounds. *Mark Twain*

I find distance lends enchantment to bagpipes – for example, the piper on one mountain, the listener on another.

William Blezard

Years ago bald musicians were thought to play more wrong notes than hairy ones.

Robert Morley

Viola players are only horn players who have lost their teeth.

Hans Richter

When people play the piano by ear, the left hand is usually quite unaware of what is going on at the upper end of the keyboard.

Virginia Graham

Too many pieces of music finish too long after the end.

Igor Stravinsky

SINGERS

I don't know anything about music. In my line you don't have to.

Elvis Presley

She's a singer we put well to the back . . . preferably in the car park.

Alan Ayckbourn

His vibrato sounded like he was driving a tractor over ploughed fields with weights tied to his scrotum.

Spike Milligan

I drove into a garage where Anthony Newley was the petrol pump, singing 'What Kind of Fuel Am I'

Eric Morecambe

I wonder why it is so easy to sing in one's bath.   *Harry Graham*

Choirs may look devout in action, but on tour they can behave like rugby football clubs.

Anthea Hall

SWEET SILENCE

Bring back the silence, the silence we once knew,
Before unending musak was endlessly piped through.

Joyce Grenfell

Names

Following complaints from devout worshippers, the Bishop of Colchester's cat 'Sherry' was hurriedly renamed 'Shandy'.

Arthur Marshall

Exam question: 'With what do you connect the name Baden-Powell?'
Answer: 'You connect it with a hyphen.'

Denis Norden

He was immensely proud of the derivation of his name from Old English *lycam*, a corpse.

Aldous Huxley

Nature

The greatest joy in Nature is the absence of man.

Bliss Carman

When a man wantonly destroys a work of man we call him a vandal; when he destroys one of the works of God we call him a sportsman.

J. W. Krutch

Nervousness

I felt more and more like a man going in to bat in his first Test Match with the score at 19 for three.

Kingsley Amis

Nursery Rhymes

Sing a song of sixpence, a pocket full of rye,
Four and twenty blackbirds baked in a pie.
When the pie was opened the birds burst into song –
These bloody micro-ovens are always going wrong.

Lambert Jeffries

Obesity

At Fat Farms or Beauty Spas one pays astronomical sums to be overexercised and underfed.

Peg Bracken

The cooler a fat man dresses, the hotter he looks.

Kin Hubbard

Don't lose your nerve
about a curve
that oughter
be shorter.

Tina Spencer Knott

The charabanc rose three feet when she got off.   *Spike Milligan*

Opera

Opera is when a guy gets stabbed in the back and instead of
bleeding he sings.

Ed Gardner

I sometimes think I'd like opera better without the singing.

John Amis

No good opera plot can be sensible, for people don't sing when
they are feeling sensible.

W. H. Auden

One can't judge Wagner's opera *Lohengrin* after a first hearing,
and I certainly have no intention of hearing it a second time.

G. A. Rossini

Parents

'I knew a girl once who called her parents by their Christian
names. She had a baby before she was 17.'

Alan Bennett

He is too experienced a parent ever to make positive promises.

Christopher Morley

Shunned are the games a parent proposes,
They prefer to squirt each other with hoses.

Ogden Nash

The child had every toy his father wanted.   *R. C. Whitten*

Parties

Anyone who sees his friends enjoying themselves at his party – has
the right to set them to work handing round the ham sandwiches.

Virginia Graham

'A few people' is always twice as many as you bargained for.

Spike Hughes

I don't have a dinner party very often; say, once every ten days.
Observer 'Sayings of the Week'

Mrs Nathalie Hambro

If you got lots of interesting and famous people together you
would have envy, competition, and rancour.

Jonathan Miller

Ernie [Wise] is the only person I know who goes to a bottle party
with a pint of milk.

Eric Morecambe

What to wear? What time to arrive? Will you know anyone? Will
you hear properly? Why have they asked you?

Robert Morley

When introducing people at social gatherings, hostesses mumble
names as if they were dirty words.

Desmond Morris

British writers have a strange way of going home from a party
before daybreak.

James Thurber

It was one of those parties where you cough twice before you
speak, and then decide not to say it after all.

P. G. Wodehouse

PARTY GAMES

It's not going to be much of a party if they don't throw toilet rolls
out of the window.

Michael Frayn

Somebody usually breaks Wedgwood at this kind of do, and hides
it under a cushion.

Eric Morecambe

It really was a very good party. No fewer than eleven of the people
who attended it never dared show their faces at the office again.

Edward Vernon

Pedestrians

Pedestrians should not cross the road at traffic lights until the little
green man appears. They can then cross in perfect safety, provided
they can cover 22 feet in three seconds.

Lambert Jeffries

There are two sorts of pedestrians – the quick and the dead.

Anon.

Peerages

When I want a peerage I shall buy one like an honest man.

Alfred Harmsworth (attrib.)

People

My window-cleaner was a lethargic menial with all the sensitivity of the Berlin Wall.

Woody Allen

He's the sort of man who will sit on a fire and then complain that his bottom is burning.

W. S. Gilbert

Only one in a hundred adults plays with toy ducks in their baths, but fifteen per cent confess to cutting their toe nails.

Martyn Harris

We are becoming a race which jogs and eats nuts.

Michael Palin

He always sees two sides to each question: his own, which is the right one, and anyone else's, which is the wrong one.

Terence Rattigan

I like both him and his wife. He is so ladylike, and she is such a perfect gentleman.

Sidney Smith

'Silent majority' usually means the noisiest minority since the Salvation Army got brass bands.

Katharine Whitehorn

UNFRIENDLY FEELING

We shared a common interest – a mutual dislike of one another.

Jack Hawkins

The retired male nurse was not liked. He measured you for a strait-jacket carefully with his eye.

Dylan Thomas

Philosophy

I have this overwhelming desire to return to the womb – any womb!

Woody Allen

'Learn to take things easily,' said a great Roman philosopher.
'Especially other people's things.'

Harry Graham

A thing should be done not only as well as possible but even better
than that.

J. H. Levy

Push will get you anywhere – except through a door marked Pull.

(Graffito)

Though statisticians in our time have never kept the score,
Man wants a great deal here below, and Woman even more.

James Thurber

Places

What Manchester thinks today, London will please herself
whether she thinks it tomorrow.

James Agate

The telephone operator told me there was no listed number for
Bodiam Castle. 'Is it new?' she asked.

Sue Arnold

'Have you ever been to Amsterdam?'
'Oh yeah, I've been to the Vatican.'
'But the Vatican's in Rome!'
'Er . . . they were doing so well in Rome they opened one in
Amsterdam.'

Woody Allen

Every time I go to the Sahara it rains. *Tim Heald*

Up north even the sparrows fly backwards to avoid getting dirt in
their eyes.

Michael Parkinson

Poetry

To those compelled to do it
    A gift for writing verse
Is not so much a blessing
    But more a kind of curse.

Roger Woddis

'He did not appear quite normal,' continued the coroner. 'He
spent a lot of his time writing poetry.'

Evening Standard

The popularity of my poem ['The Ballad of Reading Gaol'] will be largely increased by the author's painful death by starvation.

Oscar Wilde

Writing free verse is like playing tennis with the net down.

Robert Frost

Books of poems lying around are handy for killing persistent irritating flies.

Geoffrey Grigson

When you want to write something but haven't anything much to say, you can call it *vers libre*.

Lambert Jeffries

In Liverpool you can't exist as a poet just by having long hair and saying you're a poet. You have to be able to talk football as well.

Roger McGough

The fact that Lord Byron showed promise as a poet was due to the fact that he was brought up by a nurse.

Douglas Sutherland

'I remember a Canadian nurse who read aloud to me from some book or other, 'that first fine careless rupture'.

James Thurber

Politics

Democracy is the worst form of government, except for all the others.

Winston S. Churchill

A US senator, bombarded by letters written by a curmudgeonly constituent, used to reply: 'Dear Friend, I must write to tell you that some nut has been writing to me, using your name . . .'

Julian Critchley

The ideal way of opening Parliament would be to put a bomb under it and press the button.

P. G. Wodehouse

Press this button for a short political speech.

(Graffito seen on a hand-drier in a public lavatory)

A Hungarian once said to me: 'In Capitalism man exploits man. In Communism it's the other way round.

Geoffrey Green

Politicians and monkeys have one thing in common. The higher they climb, the more they reveal their unpleasant aspects.

Anon

FIRST THINGS FIRST

When the call came to me to form a Government, one of my first thoughts was that it should be a Government of which Harrow would not be ashamed.

Stanley Baldwin

Although the Queen Mother looked smashing, I felt that somebody ought to stand up for republicanism so I kept my seat when she left.

New Statesman

'The Colchester Corn Exchange will not be available this year for the General Election rally. The regular Bingo session cannot be cancelled.'

This England

Poverty

I've worked myself up from nothing to a state of extreme poverty.

Groucho Marx

Remember the poor. It costs nothing. *Josh Billings*

I was once so poor I didn't know where my next husband was coming from.

Mae West

We were so poor in those days that the mice used to set traps for us.

John Conteh

Poverty is *feeling* poor. *R. W. Emerson*

The best way to help the poor is not to become one of them.

Laing Hancock

It's easy enough to say that poverty is no crime. If it were, men wouldn't be so ashamed of it.

Jerome K. Jerome

To remain poor needs the utmost skill. *George Mikes*

Prejudice

Prejudice: a vagrant opinion without visible means of support.

Ambrose Bierce

I am free of all prejudice. I hate everyone equally. *W. C. Fields*

Presidents

In America any boy may become President. I suppose it's just one of the risks he takes.

Adlai Stevenson

There's one thing about being President – nobody can tell you when to sit down.

Dwight D. Eisenhower

Printers' Perfidy

If aunts get into your kitchen, spray the floor with paraffin.

Daily Sketch

It is considered impolite to break your beard into pieces to put in your soup.

(Book on etiquette)

Jones made a fine start by carrying his bath throughout the innings.

Denys Parsons in Irish Field

It is supposed to be lucky to pick up a pig if you see one lying on the pavement.

(Magazine article)

A startled cow fled over the elms.

(Short story)

It is probable that the great Bill Tilden bit the ball harder than any other tennis player.

Sporting Times

Hot and hungry, at lunch-time we began to look around for a suitable corpse.

(Travel article)

At Eton brothers sometimes share a room. A bursar once circulated a form to housemasters asking: 'How many rooms in your House are suitable for brothers?' Unfortunately the second *r* in the last word appeared as an *l*.

Lambert Jeffries

Progress

Progress would be wonderful if it would only stop.

Robert Musil

Last year we were poised on the edge of a precipice. This year we shall take a great leap forward.

William Davies (quoting Third World leader)

Prudence

He was oppressed by a feeling that he had gone considerably further than was prudent. Samson, as he heard the pillars of the temple begin to crack, must have felt the same.

P. G. Wodehouse

Punctuality

The trouble with being punctual is that there's nobody there to appreciate it.

Lettice Philpots

Punctuality is the virtue of the bored.

Evelyn Waugh

Quarrelling

In real life it only takes one to make a quarrel.

Ogden Nash

Quotations

In time, all humorous remarks will be ascribed to Shaw, whether he said them or not.

Nigel Rees

Even small quotations can be valuable, like raisins in a rice pudding.

Peg Bracken

I often quote myself. It adds spice to my conversation.

George Bernard Shaw

Radio

I have listened daily to 'Woman's Hour', and, frankly, some of the items are much too good for women.

Peter Freedman (quoting)

Ears are assaulted by the manic gibberish of disc jockeys whose cerebral power wouldn't equip them to engage a chimpanzee in a game of Snap.

Mike Harding

Recognition

An old lady who had never had a bank account before wanted to draw out some money, and was asked if she could identify herself. She opened her handbag, took out a mirror, and said, 'Oh yes, it *is* me.'
Lambert Jeffries

Religious Habits

White is the virginal colour, symbolising purity and innocence. Why do nuns wear black?
Dave Allen

She was an atheist and I was an agnostic. We didn't know what religion *not* to bring our children up in.
Woody Allen

A gentleman goes to church at regular intervals . . . to set a good example to those whose chance of entering the Kingdom of Heaven is less certain.
Duke of Bedford

It was the first time anyone had been known to swoon at a religious service held in November.
Arnold Bennett

Christians have burned each other, quite persuaded
That all the apostles would have done as they did.
Lord Byron

We have no authority to decide whether whale steaks are proper Friday fare.
Church Times

Monica Baldwin's *I Leap over a Wall* has strengthened me in my decision not to become a nun.
Noel Coward

ETERNITY

On the question of eternal punishment, the word 'eternal' did not appear to the elders of St Osoph's to designate a suffiently long period.
Stephen Leacock

GOD WITH A CAPITAL LETTER

Almost all religions agree that God is fond of music, sometimes of dancing, and always of processions.
Robert Morley

'There's a pretty strong case against God for cruelty to animals.'
Henry Cecil

God was satisfied with his own work, and that is fatal.
Samuel Butler

'I am not a nudist but I always say my prayers in the nude. It seems to bring me nearer to God.'
Sunday Dispatch

The story of God's love lost something in the telling when put across by the Spanish Inquisition.
Katherine Whitehorn

APOSTLES AND CLERGY

When Jesus called Peter from his boat he spoiled an honest fisherman.
George Bernard Shaw

An ex-Archbishop is a kind of extinct volcano, still able to erupt from time to time.
Geoffrey Fisher (Bishop of London)

Our Bishop allowed himself to be coerced into blessing, in full canonicals, a new Exeter multi-chain-super-store.
Arthur Marshall

'Have you ever been called to serve the Lord in heathen parts?'
'Well, I was for a short time a curate in Leeds.'
Alan Bennett

HEAVEN

'I'll tell you something. Heaven is going to be hell.' *Alan Bennett*

I don't want to go to Heaven if you have to stand all the time.
Spike Milligan

Restaurants

A man took his wife to a West End restaurant, studied the menu, and then said to the waiter: 'We've only got ten pounds to spend – what do you suggest?' 'Another restaurant, sir,' said the waiter.
Reader's Digest

There are many excellent restaurants in London. I know a particularly good one on the left-hand side.
Harry Graham

Busy restaurant on the beach of a small uninhabited island requires a manager.
Hotel & Caterer

Salesmanship

I was not a good salesman. I was attending one day to an American customer, who gushed: 'If you don't put that sweater away right now I'll buy it.' I put it away.

Michael Leapman

Schools

Matron looked after all the maids so carefully that she was reported to lock them up in cages between meals.

Patrick Campbell

This place is full of eyes, and they all belong to the headmaster.

Giles Cooper

As a schoolmaster, if I came across a boy about to run away, I would say, 'Hang on a minute, I'm coming with you'.

Arthur Marshall

I never minded the lessons. I just resented having to work terribly hard at playing.

John Mortimer

Science

As automation develops there will be more and more of Us absolutely baffled by the activities of fewer and fewer of Them.

Patrick Campbell

I find it hard to believe that the scientific mind could not, if it tried, invent a silencer for street-drills or a non-rattling underground train.

Balaam

In 1913 Science decided that there were such things as vitamins. Before 1913 people had just been eating food.   *Robert Benchley*

The line opposite the right angle in a right-angled triangle is called the hippopotamus.

Anon

HOW TO DEAL WITH AN ATOM BOMB

If an atom bomb lands near you or the dog brings one in from the garden: (1) don't touch it (2) phone the fire brigade (3) run.

Mike Harding

The Sea

No more ships for me. I'll come home by the overland route.
Lord Darnley (after a ship collision en route to Australia)

What for you want a bathroom? Have you not got the sea? (Greek house agent)
Gerald Durrell

The *Snowdonia* was one of those absolutely up-to-the-minute liners in which everything seems to be made of plastic, including the sea.
Richard Gordon

Love the sea? I dote upon it – from the beach.   *Douglas Jerrold*

A representative of the Fishing Vessel Owners agreed that men sometimes got swept overboard. 'But,' he added, 'they often get swept back again.'
Sunday Times

Sex

Sex Appeal. Please give generously.   (*Graffito*)

A lap was a good place to put a girl. She felt safer there for some reason, but was not.
Kingsley Amis

I'm as pure as the driven slush.   *Tallulah Bankhead*

The sex life of ghosts is the only kind still unexplored.
Duke of Bedford

SEXUAL ACTIVITY

'I'll make Casanova look like a celibate monk.'
R. F. Delderfield

My husband often makes love to me in the afternoon, especially on Sundays, which puts me all behind with the washing-up.'
Evening Standard

A mistress is something between a mister and a mattress.
Kevin Goldstein-Jackson

'Say when, dear.'
'After the drinks, darling.'
Kevin Goldstein-Jackson

Sex is bad for one – but it's good for two.   (*Graffito*)

'Toy manufacturers shy away from producing male dolls complete with genitalia. From a very early age my eight-year-old daughter has used modelling clay to remedy the deficiency.'

Guardian

SEX EDUCATION

Books on sex can give you a terrible inferiority complex.

Mike Harding

Sex education resulted in the fall of the Roman Empire.

Reverend John Quillan

He never washed up anything, so the kitchen was awful. It was the right background for our experiments in sex.

Mary Quant

SEX ON THE BRAIN

Freud, if really pushed, could find sexual significance in a spoonful of cold mashed potato.

Arthur Marshall

A student undergoing a word-association test was asked why a snowstorm put him in mind of sex. He replied frankly, 'Because everything does!'

Honor Tracy

Playwrights and poets and such horses' necks
Start off from anywhere and end up at sex.

Dorothy Parker

SEX GAMES

Sex is the only game that is never called off on account of darkness.

Laurence Peter

I got this black eye fighting for my girl friend's honour. She would insist on keeping it.

Anon

This world is full of people who are ready to think the worst if they see a man sneaking out of the wrong bedroom in the middle of the night.

Will Cuppy

It's not the men in my life but the life in my men that counts.

Mae West

SEX ON THE SIDE

A call-girl, wife of a colonel, told me, 'I only do this to pay my husband's surtax'.

Sunday Pictorial

In India a farm hand was caught in the act with his cow. He said he had bad eyesight and thought it was his wife.

Spike Milligan

NO SEX, PLEASE

Anne Boleyn: 'Not tonight, darling. I've got a headache.'
Henry VIII: 'We'll soon fix that.'

Mike Harding

On the night before our wedding my mother-in-law said to her daughter: 'I suppose it's too much to hope that you won't have any sexual connection with Jack?'

Jack Hawkins

Perhaps the most peculiar of all sexual aberrations is chastity.

Rémy de Gourmont

Red wine is unsuitable as an aphrodisiac. The colour is unconsciously associated with red lights and danger.

Edward Vernon

Continental people have sex life: the English have hot water bottles.

George Mikes

The ladies who used to run Holloway College insisted that, if young ladies entertained young gentlemen to tea in their rooms, then they must first put the bed outside on the landing.

Katherine Whitehorn

Shakespeare

Shake was a dramatist of note;
He lived by writing things to quote.

H. C. Bunner

Brutus seems no more than a resounding set of vocal chords wrapped up in a toga.

John Mason Brown

Ophelia, taking a quick dip after lunch, failed to allow the precautionary 1½ hours rest after a heavy meal. Shakespeare deliberately concealed the facts.

Arthur Marshall

I have seen a Lady Macbeth, evidently following the text while in the wings, make her entrance wearing a large pair of horn-rimmed spectacles.

Arthur Marshall

Lady Macbeth enters, carrying a lit-up toper.

(Foreign student)

'I heard the owl scream and the crickets cry.' (*Macbeth* II,i) Macbeth was on his way to murder Duncan when he heard the call of nature.

(Foreign student)

Shopping

Sales Psychology . . . 'We've got it – you don't want it – but you're going to buy it.'

Joyce Grenfell

Solitude

Except for four maid-servants, a page, two dogs, three gardeners, and the kitchen-clerk, Mrs Gater was alone in the Hall.

Arnold Bennett

Space

A cartoon a few years ago showed a returning astronaut being interviewed by reporters. 'Is there life on Mars?' they asked him. 'Well,' he replies, 'there's a little on Saturday nights but it's pretty dull the rest of the week.'

Adrian Berry

Speech

SPEECH IMPEDIMENTS

From my earliest days I have enjoyed an attractive impediment in my speech. I have never permitted the use of the word stammer.

Patrick Campbell

My wife has an impediment in her speech: every now and then she stops to take a breath.

Kevin Goldstein-Jackson

WORDS, WORDS, WORDS

Actions lie louder than words.   *Carolyn Wells*

I don't necessarily agree with everything I say.
Marshall McLuhan

Someone took W. S. Gilbert to task for using the word 'coyful'. 'How can anyone be full of coy?' 'I don't know,' he replied, 'but for that matter how can anyone be full of bash?'
Hesketh Pearson

We have everything in common with America nowadays, except, of course, language.
Oscar Wilde

I like knitting because it gives me something to think about while I'm talking.   *Anon*

A FEW BRIEF WORDS

The speeches to be wary of are those that begin, 'I'm not going to speak for long'.
Frank Muir

I caught his first sentence, which was that he would only detain us for a moment, but for the next fifteen minutes he baffled me completely.
P. G. Wodehouse

Most people tire of a lecture in ten minutes; clever people do it in five.
Stephen Leacock

Some people never stop to think when they're speaking; others never think to stop speaking.
Anon

TABLE TALK

'The story of your pelvis has fascinated me throughout dinner, but I think I should point out that I am a doctor of divinity.'
Richard Gordon

I remember dining with the late Lord Birkenhead. Conversation flagged until I said, 'Tell me, why didn't you get your rugger blue at Oxford?' and then he never stopped talking.
P. G. Wodehouse

Think twice before you speak – and you'll find everyone talking about something else.
Francis Rodman

HEARING A HERRING

We should turn a deaf ear to any red herring that may be drawn across our path.

Anon

Sport

SKATING AND SKIING

The thinner the ice, the more anxious everybody is to see if it will bear.

Josh Billings

The following was attached to the notice-board at a school in Esher, Surrey: 'No boy may go ice-skating on any water not passed by the headmaster.'

Daily Telegraph

Skiing? Why break my leg at 40 degrees below zero when I can fall downstairs at home?

Corey Ford

ROW, BROTHERS, ROW

It's not easy to teach a rowing man to think, because if he could think he probably wouldn't row.   *Anon*

Rowing shares with motor racing the advantage of being practised while sitting down.

Roy Plomley

The Boat Race would be much more attractive if the rules were changed to allow the boats to ram each other.

Miles Kington

BASEBALL FOR BREVITY

Baseball has the great advantage over cricket of being sooner ended.

George Bernard Shaw

Two hours is as long as an American will wait for the close of a baseball game – or anything else for that matter.

A. G. Spalding

You can't think and hit at the same time.   *Yogi Berra*

The under-privileged people of the Americas play some strange game with a bat which looks like an overgrown rolling-pin.

Fred Trueman

FOOTBALL FOR FEMALES

Football is all very well as a game for rough girls but it is hardly suitable for delicate boys.

Oscar Wilde

ANYONE FOR TENNIS?

An otherwise happily married couple may turn a mixed doubles game into a scene from *Who's Afraid of Virginia Woolf.*

Rod Laver and Bud Collins

CLIMBING

Climb every mountain,
   Ford every burn,
Suffer a thrombosis,
   End up in an urn.

Arthur Marshall

SPORTS WRITING

Sports writing is easy. You sit in front of a typewriter until little drops of blood run down your forehead.

Anon

Teaching

The pile of exercise books which I had left on the table to mark seemed as repulsive as a lump of cold suet pudding.

Balaam

The object of teaching a child is to enable him to get along without a teacher.

Elbert Hubbard

The prime function of a headmistress is to come unexpectedly round a corner and stumble on something discreditable.

Arthur Marshall

How can one imagine an intelligent man engaging in so puerile an occupation.

H. L. Mencken

'I expect you'll be becoming a schoolmaster, sir. That's what most of the gentlemen does, sir, that gets sent down for indecent behaviour.'

Evelyn Waugh

Television

TV – a device that permits people who haven't anything to do to watch people who can't do anything.

Fred Allen

The TV newsman's favourite question: 'And just how did you feel, Mrs Jones, as you watched the van run over your little boy?'

Peg Bracken

TV AND EDUCATION

TV is often a bottomless mine not only of information but also of misinformation.

Paul Johnson

I find television very educating. Every time someone turns the set on I go into another room and read a book.

Groucho Marx

Television is of great educational value. It teaches you while still young how to (*a*) kill, (*b*) rob, (*c*) embezzle, (*d*) shoot, (*e*) poison.

George Mikes

Certain television personalities give away money with great charm. Should you chance to know what the capital of France is called then you are practically certain to be sent to Majorca for a three weeks' holiday.

George Mikes

If a modern housewife finds her TV set out of action, she can't go shopping because she doesn't know what to buy.

Anon

TV AWARDS

Getting a TV award is like being kissed by someone with bad breath.

Michael Williams

Even off the set the 'Upstairs' actors never mixed with the 'Downstairs'.

Gordon Jackson (about 'Upstairs, Downstairs')

After make-up I looked like a man who had borne all the sorrows of the world on his shoulders and was about to be hanged for a crime he hadn't committed.

S. P. B. Mais

I think the hardest noise I've ever had to do was copulating rats. We had to use a lot of imagination.

Beryl Mortimer (BBC sound effects)

Having forgotten his lines, Dick Powell continued mouthing silently, and hundreds of thousands of viewers frantically twiddled their dials and phoned their repair men.

David Niven

US AND THEM

One of those smug little Talkback programmes in which the BBC has listeners' letters read out in fancy voices to give the impression that the writers are half-witted and that the BBC is always right.

Lambert Jeffries

'Laying down new guidelines', an activity favoured by the BBC, has been defined as 'trying to prevent the recurrence of a mistake that you have not admitted making'.

Oliver Pritchett

In 1966 Finnish TV announced that a new electronic device would black out all unlicensed sets. Every set in Finland was then peremptorily blacked out. Long queues formed the following morning to buy licences.

Derek Cooper

Theatre

AUDIENCES

The play was a success but the audience was a failure.

William Collier

I don't go to the theatre to see plays about rape, sodomy, and drug addiction. I can get all that at home.

Peter Cook

When you're in a flop play you're grateful to hear a cough in the theatre. It proves you're not alone.

Cedric Hardwicke

Coughing in the theatre is not a respiratory ailment. It is a criticism.

Alan Jay Lerner

We don't mind them walking out in the middle of our act. It's when they start advancing we get really worried.

Eric Morecambe

PLAYERS

A Director is a person engaged by the management to conceal the fact that the players cannot act.

James Agate

Tallulah Bankhead barged down the Nile last night as Cleopatra –
and sank.

John Mason Brown

You can pick out actors by the glazed look that comes into their
eyes when the conversation wanders away from themselves.

Michael Wilding

Because I am an actor, strangers rightly suppose I wish to talk
about myself.

Robert Morley

PLAYS

An earnest young repertory manager once said to me, in all good
faith: 'What's so nice about doing your plays in my theatre is that
the profits pay for the good ones we do.'

Terence Rattigan

My reputation as a dramatist grows with every play of mine that is
not performed.

George Bernard Shaw

It's one of those *avante-garde* plays which bring the scent of
boiling cabbage across the footlights and in which the little man in
the bowler hat turns out to be God.

P. G. Wodehouse

Travel

Three trains, cancelled to save fuel, are still running; but to show
that they are officially cancelled, no passengers are allowed to
travel on them.

Daily Worker

G. K. Chesterton's only sure way of catching a train was to miss
the train before.

Gavin Millar

If there is room for only five on a bus, you will be sixth in the
queue.

Leonard Rossiter

If you crash in a train, there you are. If you crash in a plane, where
are you?   *Anon*

DOWN UNDER

No matter which tube train you are waiting for, the wrong one
always comes first.

Miles Kington

A literary competition wickedly requested misleading advice for foreigners. A devilish one went: 'On entering an Underground train, it is the custom to shake hands with everyone present.'

Arthur Marshall

On crowded Underground platforms I invariably wait at the junction between two coaches.

Richard Gordon

Foreign travel broadens the minds of the young and the hips of the middle-aged.

Spike Hughes

We're used to being packed liked sardines in the Underground, but they might let us get our tails in before they close the doors.

Reader's Digest

Universities

I was a modest, good-humoured boy. It was Oxford that made me insufferable.

Max Beerbohm

Students at an American college were being subjected to one of those interminable, impertinent questionnaires. One of the questions was 'Are you a virgin?' I have long been fascinated by one girl's answer: 'Not yet.'

Leslie Charteris

Wales

In Wales Sunday starts early and lasts several years. *Peg Bracken*

An elderly aunt of mine once assured a friend: 'Wales is very sparsely copulated'.

W. Douglas Home

The Welsh are insistent that Welsh names must not be pronounced as they are spelt.

John Tickner

Weather

Cold? Even the gas was frozen. We had to get it out of the pipe with a corkscrew and put it in a candlestick.

Colin Howard

Sunday was one of those typical English summer days: overcast, sombre, drizzly.

Elspeth Huxley

If Shelley had been anything of a gardener he would have known that Spring is invariably far behind.

Spike Hughes

No sooner have I cleared my drive of snow than the town snow-plough comes along and shoves it all back again.

Corey Ford

There is no climate in Lima, only a sort of light drizzle.

Miles Kington

Mediterranean rain differs from British rain. You don't get it so regularly but when you do it is bigger, faster, wetter, and it bounces higher.

Frank Muir

Women

Pretty women always tended to go for horrible men.

Kingsley Amis

'I've never to this day really understood what most women think about anything.'

Alan Ayckbourn

'Dames are simple. I never met one who didn't understand a slap in the mouth.'

Humphrey Bogart

Women were not meant to live *en masse* – except in harems.

Monica Dickens

If she looks old, she's old. If she looks young, she's young. If she looks back, follow her.

Bob Hope

WOMEN IN BED

Women like you to open the door for them politely, and chuck them on the bed with no manners at all.

Jean Jerome Romanet

More women like reading in bed than lovemaking, and this in spite of the fact that a third wear no nightclothes.

Martyn Harris (analysing a questionnaire)

WOMEN AT WORK

Women's work is any tedious routine which nobody has yet invented a machine for.

Alison Macleod

Women were very rough with a launderette machine, and perhaps because it was something they didn't understand, they used a technique analogous to shouting at foreigners.

Tina Spencer Knott

Whatever women do they must do twice as well as men to be thought half as good. Luckily, this is not difficult.

Charlotte Whitton

INFINITE VARIETY

Be fair, sweet maid, and let who will be clever. If brains are wanted, I've enough for two.

P. G. Wodehouse

She looked like something that might have occurred to Ibsen in one of his less frivolous moods.

P. G. Wodehouse

When a woman behaves like a man, why doesn't she behave like a nice man?

Edith Evans

Work

The ideal job is one for which you are paid large sums for doing absolutely nothing at all.

Alan Coren

Nothing is more harmful to a spirited young man than regular work.

Richard Gordon

Idling has always been my strong point. I take no credit to myself – it is a gift.

J. K. Jerome

If two Englishman are equally eager to do a job, the job is sure to be left undone.

George Mikes

Your father was out of work. *You* are in a transitional phase between short term fluid marginal redundancy and long term possible redeployment.

Punch

Doctors are agreed that an occasional spell of work doesn't do me any lasting harm.

A. A. Milne

INSPIRING EXAMPLE

Lazy girls should be jogged into action by the news that the Duchess of Kent is doing her own nails.

This England

Writing

To write simply is as difficult as to be good.

W. Somerset Maugham

An incinerator is a writer's best friend.

Thornton Wilder

Writers, being human and usually broke, scented the easy money to be picked up in Hollywood.

David Niven

SELF-PORTRAIT

An autobiography is a book that proves that the only thing wrong with the author is his memory.

Eve Pollard

In a good autobiography you don't want facts. I shall rely on my imagination for my facts.

S. P. B. Mais

Keep a diary and someday it'll keep you.

Mae West

WRITING METHOD

Sometimes I write sober and revise drunk; sometimes I write drunk and revise sober.

Dylan Thomas

DIZZY FINGERS

A typewriter, when played with expression, is no more annoying than a piano.

Oscar Wilde

I can type /ust as well any blessedgirl if i give my mInd to oT.

A. P. Herbert

BOOKSHOP BEWILDERMENT

When an author can't find his book in the bookshops he can't understand why it isn't there. If he sees several copies of it lying around, he can't understand why they haven't been sold.

Lambert Jeffries

For one signing session in Covent Garden, not only did no one turn up – the shop didn't even know I was coming and had no copies of the book.

Tom Davies

REJECTION

We have read your manuscript with boundless delight. As it is unthinkable that we shall ever see its equal, we are to our regret compelled to return your divine composition. (Chinese rejection slip)

The Author

WRITING WRIGHTS

Why are there playwrights but no bookwrights?

Peg Bracken

Wrongs

She's desperately anxious to do the wrong thing correctly.   *Saki*

Yachts

The cruising trip was so much fun that I had to sink my yacht to make the guests go home.

F. Scott Fitzgerald

Youth

The young love to disobey – but nowadays there aren't any orders.
Jean Cocteau

Youth is a disease from which we all recover. *Dorothy Fuldheim*

Only the young die good. *Oliver Herford*

Other species have the good sense to banish their young at an early age. *John Rae*

All that the young can do for the old is to shock them and keep them up to date.

George Bernard Shaw

None of us is infalliable – not even the youngest of us.

W. H. Thompson

He had married young and kept on marrying. *P. G. Wodehouse*

I was born old and get younger every day. *H. Beerbohm Tree*